Music Secrets for the Advanced Musician
A Scarecrow Press Music Series

Music Secrets for the Advanced Musician is designed for instrumentalists, singers, conductors, composers, and other instructors and professionals in music seeking a quick set of pointers to improve their work as performers and creators of music. Easy to use and intended for the advanced musician, contributions to **Music Secrets** fill a niche for those who have moved far beyond what beginners and intermediate practitioners need. It is the perfect resource for teaching students what they need to know in order to take that next step forward and for reinforcing a set of best practices among advanced and professional musicians.

Clarinet Secrets: 52 Performance Strategies for the Advanced Clarinetist, 2nd edition, by Michele Gingras, 2006

Saxophone Secrets: 60 Performance Strategies for the Advanced Saxophonist, by Tracy Lee Heavner, 2013

Saxophone Secrets

60 Performance Strategies for the Advanced Saxophonist

Tracy Lee Heavner

Music Secrets for the Advanced Musician

THE SCARECROW PRESS, INC.
Lanham • Toronto • Plymouth, UK
2013

Published by Scarecrow Press, Inc.
A wholly owned subsidary of The Rowman & Littlefield Publishing Group, Inc.
4501 Forbes Boulevard, Suite 200, Lanham, Maryland 20706
www.rowman.com

10 Thornbury Road, Plymouth PL6 7PP, United Kingdom

British Library Cataloguing in Publication Information Available

Library of Congress Cataloging-in-Publication Data

Heavner, Tracy Lee, 1961–
  Saxophone secrets : 60 performance strategies for the advanced saxophonist / Tracy
Lee Heavner.
     pages cm. — (Music secrets for the advanced musician)
  Includes bibliographical references and index.
  ISBN 978-0-8108-8465-6 (pbk. : alk. paper) — ISBN 978-0-8108-8466-3 (ebook) 1.
Saxophone—Instruction and study. I. Title.
  MT500.H43 2013
  788.7'193—dc23
                                                                          2012042231

∞™ The paper used in this publication meets the minimum requirements of
American National Standard for Information Sciences—Permanence of
Paper for Printed Library Materials, ANSI/NISO Z39.48-1992.

Printed in the United States of America.

To Adolphe Sax.
Thank you for inventing such a marvelous instrument
that has allowed me and countless others
a unique means of musical expression,
greatly enriching our lives.

Contents

Preface

The purpose of this book is to provide advancing saxophonists with performance secrets that will assist in their musical development. The 60 strategies presented in the book, many of which were discovered by the author through personal teaching and performance experience, introduce a wide variety of techniques that, when mastered, will greatly improve a saxophonist's performance ability. Some of the strategies discuss the fundamental concepts needed for correct embouchure, breathing, and finger technique while others present knowledge in more advanced techniques used in both classical and jazz styles. This book is designed to be "hands on" with the strategies being read first, then practiced, and finally incorporated into performance.

Strategies presented in chapters 1 and 2 introduce knowledge regarding various brands of saxophones, mouthpieces, ligatures, and reeds. This knowledge is essential for saxophonists since acquiring and maintaining the proper equipment is the first step to becoming an advanced performer.

Chapters 3, 4, 5, and 6 present strategies for developing and improving embouchure, tone, articulation, and finger technique. With this information, saxophonists can analyze their own approach in these areas and make adjustments if necessary. Additional exercises are also included in these chapters for saxophonists to further develop their technique.

Chapters 7 and 8 introduce strategies for developing the altissimo register and extended saxophone techniques such as circular breathing, slap tonguing, flutter tonguing, and multiphonics. These techniques are essential for saxophonists who desire to play contemporary, classical, jazz, or commercial music.

Chapter 9 contains strategies that introduce popular jazz techniques to assist classical saxophonists who also desire to be accomplished performers in jazz and commercial styles. Unlike other woodwind instrumentalists, saxophonists are sometimes expected to be proficient in performing classical, jazz, and commercial musical styles due to the nature and history of the instrument.

Chapter 10 introduces strategies to assist saxophonists when traveling by presenting information on flight cases, items to be carried in the case, booking flights, and boarding aircraft with a saxophone and also suggestions to help prepare for a performance.

By reading, understanding, and utilizing the strategies presented in this book, advancing saxophonists will dramatically improve their performance skills in the shortest period of time with the minimum amount of practice.

CHAPTER 1

Saxophones, Mouthpieces, and Equipment Strategies

SECRET 1: SELECTING A SAXOPHONE

There are many brands of saxophones currently being produced varying greatly in quality and price. Within their brand, most saxophone manufacturers also produce several different models in order to meet the needs of performers at various stages of development. Student models, designed for beginning saxophonists, are the least expensive but also contain the least amount of craftsmanship. Intermediate models, designed for advancing performers, are more expensive because they are made using better materials and more craftsmanship and contain a few extra features. Professional models, used mainly by advanced saxophonists, are the most expensive and are made using the best materials. They also contain the most craftsmanship and are equipped with extra features not included on less-expensive models.

A majority of saxophonists learn to play using a student model, but as they improve, they upgrade to an intermediate instrument. Some saxophonists improve to a point that they consider purchasing a professional-quality instrument dependent upon their budget and performance goals.

When selecting a saxophone to purchase, some factors to consider are the instrument's tone quality, intonation, response, durability, and price. Recommendations from saxophone teachers as well as professional performers are also important factors to consider when determining which saxophone would be the best choice.

Popular Saxophone Brands and Models

Although there are many saxophone brands used by professional saxophonists, the two most popular are Selmer and Yamaha. Selmer saxophones have a long tradition as being the favorite of many professional performers, especially the Selmer Mark VI model, which was manufactured from 1954 through 1973. Currently Selmer's two highest-quality instruments are the Selmer Paris Series III, preferred by classical saxophonists, and the Selmer Paris Reference 54, which was designed after the Selmer Mark VI and is preferred by jazz performers. These instruments are used by many saxophonists and are excellent professional instruments.

In recent years, the Yamaha brand has become very popular with upcoming performers and even some seasoned Selmer artists. Yamaha also produces two professional-quality instruments, one designed primarily for classical performers and the other for jazz. The Yamaha Custom 875 EX saxophone is a professional model saxophone that produces a rich, dark tone that is excellent for performing classical music. For performing in the jazz style, Yamaha produces the Yamaha Z model, which has a brighter tone and is endorsed by many jazz saxophonists.

In addition to Selmer and Yamaha, several other saxophones brands that have reached a level of popularity, especially among jazz saxophonists, are Yanagisawa, Keilwerth, and Cannonball.

Saxophone Finishes

In addition to the brand and model, another factor to consider when selecting a saxophone is the finish. The finish is a coating used to cover the bare brass of the saxophone, protecting it from the elements and also providing a more appealing appearance.

The type of finish will also have an effect on the tone. In addition to protecting the instrument and giving it a beautiful look, the finish also restricts the natural resonance of the brass and, as a result, darkens the tone. Saxophones with the brightest tone are usually ones coated with no finish, which allows the brass to resonate freely. As a result, these instruments are very popular with jazz and commercial saxophonists even though their appearance may not be as appealing as other finished saxophones.

When ranking the effect of finishes on tone quality, performers will discover that saxophones with a clear lacquer finish have the brightest tone, followed by nickel, black lacquer, silver, and finally gold. Saxophones finished in gold plating, which is the thickest saxophone finish and also the most expensive, will have the darkest tone with all other factors remaining equal.

When selecting a saxophone finish, both the appearance and tonal effect should be considered. However, saxophonists who choose a finish based more on appearance than tone quality can still influence the brightness or darkness of their tone. By adjusting the embouchure and selecting the appropriate mouthpiece, ligature, and reed, saxophonists can brighten or darken their tone, fine-tuning it for each performance situation.

Choosing a Specific Saxophone

When selecting a saxophone, performers should research various brands, models, and finishes using the Internet; learn about equipment used by top professional saxophonists; get recommendations from saxophone teachers; and finally test-play a variety of saxophones at larger music stores who have them in stock.

When the saxophone brand, model, and finish have been decided, it is time to choose the specific instrument to purchase. Theoretically, saxophones of the same brand, model, and finish should play identically to each other, but unfortunately this is not the case. Depending upon the brand and model, there can be quite a difference between individual instruments. The only way to find the best instrument is to test-play several identical saxophones using the same mouthpiece, ligature, and reed. Hopefully, a local music store will have several saxophones to choose from and practice rooms available to test-play them.

If a local store does not have the desired saxophones in stock, some online instrument companies may ship several instruments at once for individuals to try for a short period of time. Although this is not the most convenient way to select an instrument, serious saxophonists should always have several instruments to choose from.

When several identical instruments have been acquired, each should be test-played for tone, intonation, and response. When playing each instrument, saxophonists should listen carefully to see which instrument has the best tone and also check the intonation throughout the entire range of the instrument using a tuner. Although no saxophone is built perfectly in tune, only minor embouchure adjustments should be necessary to correct notes that are out of tune. Saxophonists should also check the instrument for response in the low, middle, high, and altissimo registers.

If possible, each instrument should be recorded while being test-played. It is often easier to determine which instrument sounds best using a recording since this allows performers to focus their full attention on each example rather than trying to play and listen at the same time. Many times if three saxophones are tested, one will stand out as being the worst and can be easily eliminated. However, the other two instruments may be very close in playing characteristics. In this situation, it may take several more test-plays to determine which instrument is best. In some cases, it may be obvious that one instrument plays far better than the other two, making the choice of which instrument to purchase a simple one.

If a satisfactory instrument is found at a local store but the price is higher than buying the same instrument online, the store manager should be asked if the online price can be matched. Many times the local store will sell the instrument for the discounted online price.

SECRET 2: SELECTING A CLASSICAL SAXOPHONE MOUTHPIECE

When striving to produce a good saxophone tone, one of the most crucial pieces of equipment is the mouthpiece. There are many brands of saxophone mouthpieces being manufactured using a variety of materials and encompassing a wide price range and designed for performers at all levels of development. Beginning saxophonists usually play the stock mouthpieces sold with their student model saxophones. These synthetic mouthpieces are inexpensive, mass-produced, and primarily designed to produce the basic sound. As a saxophonist progresses, the stock mouthpiece is usually replaced by one made of ebonite, also known as hard rubber. These mouthpieces, which are somewhat more expensive, are made of a better material and with more craftsmanship, allowing the performer to attain a better tone. They also come in a variety of tip openings, facings, and chamber sizes, providing saxophonists with more opportunities to find a mouthpiece that better suits their particular playing style. Many professional saxophonists perform on hand-finished, hard rubber mouthpieces that allow for maximum expression and individuality.

Tip Openings, Facings, and Chamber Sizes

When selecting a mouthpiece, the tip opening, facing, and chamber size should carefully be considered. The tip opening is the distance between the tip of the reed and the tip of the mouthpiece. Mouthpieces with small tip openings are easier to control and have a more stable pitch but require a harder reed. As the tip opening increases in size, control becomes more difficult, the pitch is more flexible, and a softer reed must be used.

The mouthpiece facing is the distance between the tip of the mouthpiece and the point where the reed and the mouthpiece separate. The longer the facing, the more mouthpiece the saxophonist will need to take into the mouth in order to line up the lower teeth with the position where the reed and mouthpiece separate. Due to this fact, a medium facing usually works best for most performers.

The mouthpiece chamber is the internal cavity inside the mouthpiece, and its design has a direct effect on tone and response. The chamber can be small, medium, or large in size and have a variety of shapes from round to rectangular. A small, rectangular chamber will produce a brighter tone with more power. As the chamber size increases and becomes more round in shape, the tone will become darker and less powerful.

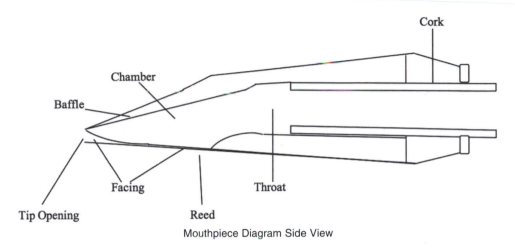

Mouthpiece Diagram Side View

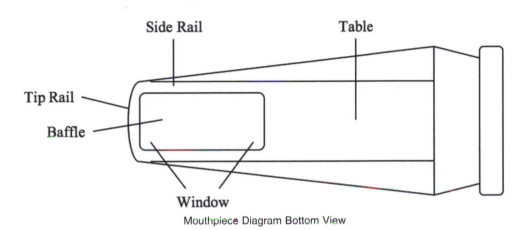

Mouthpiece Diagram Bottom View

Classical Saxophone Tone

When Adolphe Sax invented the saxophone, he designed the mouthpiece with a large, round chamber that produced a dark, round sound with little or no edge. His tonal concept gave the saxophone a beautiful solo voice that was also desirable in ensemble performance because it allowed the saxophone to blend properly with other instruments of the orchestra and symphonic band.

With the formation of the jazz big band saxophone section in the 1930s, the design of saxophone mouthpieces changed, giving jazz saxophonists the ability to play with more power and edge in their sound. This trait also carried over into the classical arena as classical saxophonists adopted this tonal style to some extent.

Modern-day classical saxophonists still strive for a warm, dark sound but with the additional power afforded by the change in mouthpiece design.

Before attempting to select a classical mouthpiece, the saxophonist must first develop a classical tonal concept. This concept can be developed by listening to prominent classical saxophonists perform in live concerts, lessons, master classes, and recordings. After this concept has been developed, mouthpieces can then be test-played to see which one allows the previously established tonal concept to be achieved.

Classical Saxophone Mouthpieces

There are numerous saxophone mouthpieces designed specifically for playing classical music. These mouthpieces are usually made of hard rubber, have small tip openings, and are played with medium to hard reeds. Their chamber design is somewhat round in nature with several facings and tip openings available to meet the requirements of various performers.

In addition to producing a good tone, several other performance aspects should also be considered when choosing a classical mouthpiece. Good response, intonation, and control in all registers; amount of air resistance; and whether the mouthpiece is reed friendly are all important factors to consider when selecting a mouthpiece.

Mouthpiece response, control, and intonation in all registers, especially in the low and upper range of the instrument, should be carefully examined. Many mouthpieces will sound great in the middle register, but when playing in the extreme registers, both low and high, response may be poor. Also some mouthpieces, while producing a good tone on certain pitches, can be hard to control due to their chamber design, tip opening, and facing. The result can be problems with squeaking, intonation, and embouchure fatigue.

Air resistance and reed friendliness are two other considerations that should not be ignored. The amount of air resistance a mouthpiece creates while being blown is an important factor in how comfortable it will feel when being played. Some saxophonists prefer a free-blowing mouthpiece with little resistance while others like more air resistance.

Reed friendliness refers to the ability of a mouthpiece to produce a good tone on a variety of reeds that have the same strength number but are not exactly equal in reed hardness. Since the strength number given to a reed by the manufacturer is only an approximation of how hard the reed really is, saxophonists need a mouthpiece that can play reeds that vary slightly in strength in order to avoid problems when rotating or switching reeds before a performance. Having a reed-friendly mouthpiece will give the saxophonist the peace of mind of knowing that if a reed is damaged or dies before a big performance, another reed can be easily substituted in its place.

Several popular classical saxophone mouthpieces used by professional performers and teachers are the Eugene Rousseau New Classic, Selmer Paris C* S80 or S90, Selmer Paris Soloist, and the Vandoren Optimum. For saxophonists who prefer the original tonal concept of Adolphe Sax, the Sigurd Rascher mouthpiece is designed to produce this sound. A sketch of the original Adolphe Sax mouthpiece can be seen below.

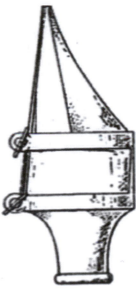

Adolphe Sax
Mouthpiece. *Courtesy of
Raschermouthpieces.com*

Selecting a Classical Saxophone Mouthpiece

When selecting a classical saxophone mouthpiece, the performer must first narrow down the choices since it is difficult to play every brand of mouthpiece made. This can be done by researching various mouthpieces using the Internet, researching mouthpiece brands and models played by prominent saxophonists, getting recommendations from saxophone teachers, and finally test-playing mouthpieces at larger music stores that have them in stock.

If the local store does not have the requested mouthpieces in stock, some online stores may ship several mouthpieces at once for individuals to try. Although this is not the most convenient way to select a mouthpiece, serious saxophonists should test-play many mouthpieces before deciding on the specific one to purchase. When ordering mouthpieces online, some stores have a return policy that will allow the performer to keep the mouthpieces for up to 30 days. This is very helpful since the saxophonist can practice and perform on the mouthpieces in a variety of situations and venues such as rehearsals, sectionals, and ensemble and solo performances.

By playing the mouthpieces for several weeks, most of the time the saxophonist can be sure that the mouthpiece selected is the best one. If possible, each mouthpiece should be recorded while being test-played. It is often easier to determine which one sounds best using a recording since this allows saxophonists to focus their full attention on each example rather than trying to play and listen at the same time.

When test-playing any mouthpiece, saxophonists should protect it from marks or scratches caused by the teeth or ligature. If a mouthpiece is damaged in any way when it is test-played, the saxophonist may have to buy the mouthpiece even though he or she may not want to. To ensure that the mouthpiece is not damaged when being test-played, a mouthpiece cushion or tape should be placed on the mouthpiece beak to protect it from teeth marks.

To protect the body of the mouthpiece, a leather or fabric ligature in the Rovner style should be used so the mouthpiece will not be scratched when the ligature is placed on it. By following this advice, many mouthpieces may be test-played without damage. If a satisfactory mouthpiece is found at a local store but the price is higher than buying the same mouthpiece online, the store manager should be asked if the online price can be matched. Many times the local store will sell the mouthpiece for the discounted online price.

SECRET 3: SELECTING A JAZZ SAXOPHONE MOUTHPIECE

Jazz mouthpieces were first designed to meet the needs of saxophonists performing in jazz big bands of the 1930s. When performing big band music, saxophonists needed a mouthpiece that would provide more volume, projection, and edge, allowing them to match the sound produced by the brass section. Mouthpieces designed up to this time had a large, round chamber that produced a softer, darker sound typically desired by classical saxophonists. During the 1930s, mouthpiece manufacturers started experimenting with the size and shape of the mouthpiece chamber, tip openings, facings, and materials mouthpieces were made from. By designing the mouthpiece chamber with a more narrow and rectangular shape, increasing the tip opening, and sometimes using metal as the construction material, mouthpieces grew more powerful with more projection and edge.

Jazz Saxophone Tone

Unlike classical saxophone tone, the tonal concept for contemporary jazz and commercial music can vary widely among performers. This may be a result of each saxophonist trying to develop a personal, identifiable sound that will set him or her apart from other performers. However, in general, jazz saxophonists have a more powerful, brighter tone that contains more edge than classical performers.

Jazz saxophonists usually begin developing their sound by first emulating their favorite artist in both tone and playing style, many times purchasing the exact mouthpiece of the performer they like. However, as they progress, they tend to develop their own personal sound, which may be very similar to the tone they started with or it could be entirely different. As this evolution takes place, the saxophonist may change mouthpieces several times trying to find the one that best matches his or her tonal concept at that moment in time. Eventually most jazz saxophonists find a mouthpiece they are satisfied with and direct their focus on other aspects of performance.

Jazz Saxophone Mouthpieces

There are a wide variety of jazz saxophone mouthpieces being manufactured using materials such as hard rubber, stainless steel, or other types of metal alloy. In addition, some manufacturers offer saxophonists a choice of hard rubber or metal when choosing a mouthpiece. While this is important because saxophonists usually have a preference for the feel of either hard rubber or metal, it should be noted that the design of the mouthpiece is the most important factor in sound production, not the material from which the mouthpiece is made.

When examining jazz mouthpieces, saxophonists will notice that their tip openings are larger than classical mouthpieces and require the use of a softer reed. Their chambers are also designed to produce more volume, power, and edge; many mouthpiece brands offer models with a choice of small, which is the brightest; medium; and large chambers. Some mouthpiece brands such as Runyon provide a removable spoiler, which is a baffle with small metal reeds that can be attached inside the mouthpiece, allowing the performer the ability to add even more edge and volume to the performer's sound.

For some saxophonists, vintage mouthpieces are highly desirable because they produce a tone quality from an era gone by. These mouthpieces, which are no longer manufactured, play quite differently from new ones, even those with the same brand and model name. They are also hard to find and have a much higher price tag. However, if a vintage mouthpiece allows a saxophonist to attain the ideal tone, the time spent searching for one and the higher price are well worth the extra effort.

Some popular jazz hard rubber mouthpieces are Beechler, Freddie Gregory, Jody Jazz, Claude Lakey, Meyer, Otto Link, Selmer Soloist, and Vandoren. Popular metal mouthpieces are Beechler Bellite, Berg Larsen, Bobby Dukkoff, Dave Guardala, Otto Link, Peter Ponsol, and Runyon. Many prominent smooth jazz alto saxophonists have gravitated toward metal mouthpieces, especially the Beechler Bellite 7 Model.

Selecting a Jazz Saxophone Mouthpiece

When selecting a jazz mouthpiece, the same procedure that was used in selecting a classical mouthpiece detailed in Secret 2 should be followed. However, it is even more important for saxophonists to test-play jazz mouthpieces in a variety of musical situations and venues since jazz and commercial music span a broad range of musical styles.

There are many choices available when selecting a jazz mouthpiece, which can be both a good and bad thing. With so many mouthpieces to choose from, saxophonists can feel confident that they will find one that meets their needs. However, it may take a lot of time and effort test-playing numerous models until that perfect mouthpiece is found. Some saxophonists are fortunate and find a suitable mouthpiece right away while others search for a long time. In addition, as performers develop, they sometimes outgrow the mouthpiece they selected and the search starts over again. It is highly suggested that saxophonists find a suitable mouthpiece and stay with it, focusing their efforts on other important aspects of playing.

SECRET 4: CUSTOMIZING A SAXOPHONE MOUTHPIECE

Although there are a wide variety of mouthpieces currently being manufactured, some saxophonists may still not be able to find one that perfectly suits their needs. In this case, a custom mouthpiece may be the answer. A custom mouthpiece is one that is created especially for a specific performer based on his or her needs, desires, and playing specifications. Sometimes a custom mouthpiece is newly created from a saxophone mouthpiece blank, while other times an already existing mouthpiece is customized to meet a saxophonist's performance specifications.

Custom Mouthpieces

There are numerous craftsmen who specialize in making mouthpieces for saxophonists based on their playing style, reed selection, instrument selection, and a variety of other personal factors. After determining which craftsman will be used through an Internet search or based on recommendations, the saxophonist must contact this person to discuss the project. This can be done over the phone, but if possible, a personal visit to the shop often works best. At this time, the saxophonist should disclose what the current problems are with the existing mouthpiece; in other words, what the mouthpiece is doing that is not liked and what the mouthpiece is not doing that the performer wants it to. In addition to this information, the saxophonist should also let the craftsman know what other equipment is currently being used including the reed brand and strength, ligature, and saxophone. Using this information, the mouthpiece maker can determine if customizing an existing mouthpiece will solve the performer's problems or if creating a new one is the best solution.

If a new mouthpiece is warranted, one will be made using a mouthpiece blank, or *shell* as they are sometimes called, that addresses the concerns of the performer. When making the new mouthpiece, the craftsman will design the chamber in conjunction with the facing to create a mouthpiece with optimal sound and response. This process is known as *voicing* the mouthpiece. After the mouthpiece is completed, it will be test-played by the maker to ensure that it is playing correctly. However, if for some reason the owner upon playing is not happy with the results, some craftsmen will make additional modifications if requested.

If customizing an existing mouthpiece is the best remedy, the craftsman will first check the mouthpiece table to make sure it is flat. Second, the facing and window of the mouthpiece will be checked to make sure all measurements on each side of the window are accurate. Next the width of the side and tip rails will be measured. If any measurements are off, the craftsman will make the necessary adjustments. A fourth step is to check the contour of the inside of the mouthpiece and re-voice it if necessary. Finally a light polish and cleaning of the mouthpiece will be completed before the job is finished.

Choosing to have a new custom mouthpiece made or to have an existing one altered can be an expensive undertaking depending upon the material the mouthpiece is made from, who the craftsman is, and how long it takes to complete the job. However, if a saxophonist cannot find a suitable mouthpiece already being manufactured, a customized one is well worth the expense.

SECRET 5: MOUTHPIECE CUSHIONS

Mouthpiece cushions are small, round or oval-shaped patches used by some saxophonists to protect the mouthpiece from teeth marks and wear. They are placed on the beak of the mouthpiece and held in place by an adhesive backing that allows them to be applied and removed several times before losing their grip.

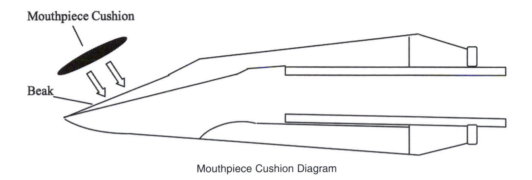

Mouthpiece Cushion Diagram

Cushions are either dark or clear in color and come in a variety of thicknesses, with the darker cushions being the thickest. Dark patches are soft and around 80 mm thick, while clear patches are harder and thinner, around 40 mm thick. Mouthpiece cushions are inexpensive, waterproof, and an excellent way to protect the mouthpiece.

Other Benefits

In addition to protecting the mouthpiece from teeth marks, cushions also protect the top teeth from excessive enamel wear. In addition, some saxophonists complain about annoying vibrations made by the reed and mouthpiece that are felt in the top teeth. These vibrations can cause saxophonists to experience an uncomfortable feeling when playing and even pain similar to a toothache. Mouthpiece cushions can provide a solution to this problem since they dampen the mouthpiece vibrations and also provide a softer, more comfortable surface for the top teeth to rest upon.

Cushions also provide the saxophonist with more grip on the mouthpiece, which increases embouchure stability. This is especially true for performers who have irregular top teeth. For these saxophonists, who are not satisfied with the feel of even the thickest cushions, two dark patches can be stacked one on top of the other to double the thickness. If this combination is too thick, then one dark cushion can be combined with one clear cushion, which is thinner, to produce the proper feel.

Attaching a cushion to the beak of a mouthpiece dampens its tonal resonance, producing a darker sound. For some saxophonists this is a desired effect, especially those who play in the classical style. However, for saxophonists who are striving for a brighter tone, this effect hinders their efforts. For saxophonists who like the comfort a cushion provides but also want a brighter sound, the solution is to cut the cushion in half. This reduces the amount of surface contact between the mouthpiece and cushion, producing a brighter tone while also providing the saxophonist with the comfort desired. As an added benefit, the saxophonist now has twice the amount of cushions originally purchased.

There are a variety of mouthpiece cushion manufacturers that produce patches in several shapes, sizes, and thicknesses. BG, Runyon, Yamaha, Giardinelli, Leblanc, and Vandoren all produce mouthpiece cushions, which are sold in packages of two, four, or six.

SECRET 6: SELECTING A SAXOPHONE LIGATURE

The saxophone ligature is considered to be an important factor in tone production since it is in direct contact with the mouthpiece and reed. The purpose of the ligature is to hold the reed snugly to the mouthpiece so it does not move but at the same time allow the reed and mouthpiece to vibrate freely, promoting a tone rich in harmonics and good response.

In reality, the type of ligature used, as long as it is functioning correctly, does not have a significant effect on the overall tone produced. It is very difficult to actually hear a tonal difference in a saxophonist's sound by changing only the type of ligature used. However, the ligature does have an effect on the way the reed "feels" to the saxophonist when it is played and also on the response of the instrument. Therefore, it is important to have a ligature that actively promotes the vibration of the mouthpiece and reed.

Ligature Materials and Styles

There are many ligatures being manufactured in numerous styles and made from a variety of materials. Brass, fabric, gold, nickel, leather, nylon, plastic, rubber, silver, and wood are just some of the materials used in saxophone ligatures. There are also various ligature styles ranging from a basic ring with no screws to more complex designs using pressure plates and screws. When determining which ligature will work best, all of these factors should be carefully considered.

The basic standard ligature that accompanies most stock mouthpieces is made from thin metal and has two screws on the underside of the mouthpiece. These ligatures, which are the least expensive models, are not very good in promoting reed vibration and can be easily broken. Most saxophonists when replacing the stock mouthpiece with a new one will also purchase a new ligature that is well made and assists the new mouthpiece in producing the best tone possible.

Ligature Placement

When placing the ligature on the mouthpiece, special care should be taken so the reed is not damaged. During this process, the reed should be placed on the mouthpiece first and held in place by the thumb. The ligature is then carefully slipped over the mouthpiece and reed, making sure not to touch the tip of the reed. Also, it is important to make sure the ligature is lined up exactly in the center of the reed, only touching the bark and not the filed portion. By experimenting with the placement of the ligature, saxophonists will usually find a spot that works best for producing optimum reed response. Once the ligature is placed correctly, the screws may be tightened but only enough to hold the reed snugly in place. If the screws are tightened too much, reed response will be inhibited and there is also a chance of breaking the ligature.

Two-Screw, Inverted Ligatures

There are several popular ligatures that use a two-screw, inverted design with the two screws on top. Rico produces the H ligature, a retro version of the famous Harrison ligature. This ligature holds the reed in place from the underside of the mouthpiece with four single contact points located on a metal, H-shaped band.

Rico H Ligature. *Courtesy of Ricoreeds.com*

Another metal ligature that follows this design, both in standard and inverted models, is the Bonade. This ligature is made from either nickel or brass and is designed to hold the reed in place by two ridges running parallel with the reed. Special care in this design ensures the sides of the reed do not touch the ligature, improving vibration and response.

The Oleg Olegature is also similar in design with two inverted screws, but is slightly different in the way the reed is held to the mouthpiece. This ligature holds the reed in place by a metal mesh band, which applies equal pressure to the entire surface of the reed. Since a mesh band is used, this ligature can also be produced in many different sizes, allowing it to fit a variety of hard rubber and metal mouthpieces.

Horizontal One-Screw, Inverted, Leather/Fabric Ligatures

There are several popular ligatures made from leather or fabric that use a one-screw, inverted design with the screw on top. Rovner and BG produce ligatures in this style, both standard and inverted, in which a band of leather is used to wrap around the reed, applying equal surface pressure to the reed. Although this ligature promotes good reed vibration, it produces a darker sound due to the large amount of surface contact between the leather and the reed. To provide saxophonists with more options, this ligature comes in several different models with various portions of leather removed from the band. This feature decreases the amount of surface contact between the ligature and the reed, producing a brighter sound.

Rovner Ligature. *Courtesy of Rovnerproducts.com*

Vertical One-Screw, Standard, Pressure Plate Ligatures

Another popular ligature uses a one-screw, standard ligature design in which the reed is held in place by a pressure plate. Vandoren Optimum Series ligatures follow this design and come with three different interchangeable pressure plates, each with its own unique pattern of reed contact points. One of the plates has four small points that minimally contact the reed, while another uses two solid thin lines, one on the top and bottom of the plate running across the reed. A third plate uses two solid ridges that run parallel with the reed. Due to the difference in contact point design, each plate produces a different amount of reed vibration, thus altering the harmonics.

The Ultimate Ligature by Francois Louis also follows this design but with several differences. Very similar to the Winslow ligature that is no longer in production, this ligature surrounds the mouthpiece using a metal frame with four brass tubes as contact points. One vertical screw is used to apply tension to a single pressure plate.

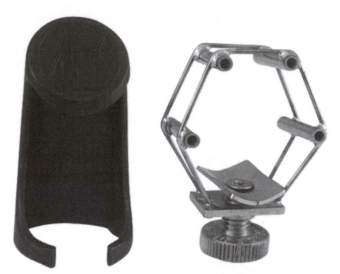

Ultimate Ligature by Francois Louis. *Courtesy of Francois-Louis.com*

Ring Ligatures

This style of ligature is very simple in design and basically consists of a single ring made of metal, rubber, or wood that slides over the mouthpiece and reed. Bois makes two models following this design, the Bois Classique and the Bois Excellente. The ligatures contain an inner rubber O-ring that prevents the ligature from scratching the mouthpiece and holds it in place. As a result of this design, these ligatures only touch the outside edges of the reed and the backside of the mouthpiece, increasing reed vibration and harmonics.

Another ligature that follows this design is the Jody Jazz Ring Ligature. It is made from brass and designed to fit the Jody Jazz DV series mouthpieces. This ligature does not contain an O-ring but uses a machine-tapered brass ring to hold the reed in place by only touching its sides and the top of the mouthpiece.

Selecting a Ligature

When selecting a ligature, it is important to first research a variety of ligatures through the Internet, ask for recommendations from saxophone teachers, and observe what top professional performers are using. After narrowing down the choices based on the information gathered, different ligatures should be test-played using the same mouthpiece, reed, and instrument. If the ligatures requested are not available at a local music store, they can be ordered online and, depending on the store's return policy, could be test-played for up to 30 days before they have

Bois Excellente Ligature. *Courtesy of Boisligatures.com*

to be returned. Although this may not be the most convenient way to gain access to the ligatures, it allows the saxophonist an extended period to try them in a variety of practice and performance situations. Although a big difference in tone may not be able to be heard between ligatures, the saxophonist will certainly be able to feel which ligature produces the greatest reed vibration and response. By test-playing the ligatures for an extended time, the saxophonist will also have a better chance of selecting the best ligature for his or her playing style and mouthpiece setup.

SECRET 7: PALM KEY RISERS

For some saxophonists, developing palm key technique is a challenge. These keys, used to finger the notes of the upper register, specifically high D, E♭, E, and F, can feel awkward to many performers since to depress these notes, the left-hand palm must be used. In addition, high E and F are notes whose fingerings require a combination of the left-hand palm along with fingers from both the left and right hands.

To compound matters, many saxophonists do not have the embouchure strength to work on these fingerings for extended periods of time since these notes are at the top of the normal written range for saxophone. Combine these factors with the fact that some saxophones are built with palm keys that are hard to reach and it is easy to see why palm key technique is lacking in many saxophonists.

The best solution to poor palm key technique is slow, perfect practice while keeping the hands close to the keys. However, for saxophonists who feel that the palm keys on their particular instrument are poorly designed or hard to reach, a solution, in addition to slow, perfect practice, may be the use of palm key risers.

Palm key risers are usually made from rubber and fit over the existing left-hand palm keys, increasing their height and making them easier to reach. In addition, some saxophonists place risers on the right-hand side keys for the same purpose. Depending on the design of the saxophone, palm key risers may increase speed, accuracy, and comfort, especially over fast musical passages, by reducing the amount of movement required to depress the keys. For performers who have repetitive strain injury, palm key risers may also provide some relief.

Two popular palm key riser manufacturers are Runyon and Oleg. Runyon produces inexpensive risers made of rubber that slip over existing palm keys. Oleg produces more expensive risers made of cast metal that attach to the instrument with set screws. Both of these products are good solutions to a poorly designed saxophone and can assist in the development of palm key technique.

Concerns

One concern with palm key risers is that they only come in one size for each saxophone type. This standard sizing may be too big or small for some performers' hands, and since the risers slip over existing palm keys, they may not be held securely in place. To overcome these issues, saxophonists sometimes hand-make their own risers out of cork and sand them down to the perfect size. However, cork risers and rubber palm key risers that do not fit well must be glued to the instrument, which may damage the finish of the saxophone if the riser is removed.

Sugru

For saxophonists who would like to make their own palm key risers but are concerned about using cork and gluing it to their instrument, there is a new alternative call Sugru. Sugru feels like modeling clay but is actually silicone rubber that can be shaped for up to 30 minutes once it has been removed from its packaging and exposed to air. After curing for 24 hours at room temperature, Sugru is a soft, flexible, waterproof, temperature-resistant material that will adhere to many different surfaces including aluminum, steel, ceramics, glass, wood, and some plastics.

Sugru is inexpensive and can be easily purchased from online stores. It comes in a variety of colors and is often sold in a bundle of 12 individually wrapped packs with five grams of Sugru in each pack. The shelf life for Sugru is approximately six months so it is essential to use it before the expiration date listed on the package. However, if placed in the refrigerator, the shelf life can be extended another six months. Sugru, once cured, can be easily removed and will not damage most surfaces. Since Sugru is a nonslip material, it is easy to grip and perfect for making palm key risers.

Sugru Packages. *Courtesy of Sugru.com*

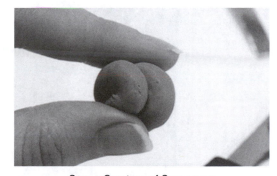

Sugru. *Courtesy of Sugru.com*

If saxophonists are not satisfied with the palm key risers currently available for sale, they may decide to custom-make their own using Sugru. In the first step of this process, saxophonists should wash their hands and also wipe the palm keys to be altered with a soft cloth to remove any dirt or oil. Next, Sugru can be taken from its package, keeping in mind that it will begin to set up in about 30 minutes.

The third step is to place some Sugru on a palm key and mold it into the desired shape making sure that the top and underside of the key is encased in Sugru. A thin layer of Sugru is placed on the underside of the key to promote a stronger bond and prevent the riser from slipping off unexpectedly. There is no need to remove the palm key from the saxophone during the application process since there will be plenty of room to size and shape the Sugru with the key left in place. Next, the saxophonist should check the molded Sugru riser within the 30-minute time limit for correct size and shape and make adjustments if needed.

Finally, the riser should be allowed to cure for at least 24 hours before playing. Depending on the thickness of the riser, a longer time may be necessary to allow the riser to cure fully in the center. After the riser is fully cured, it should be test-played to ensure it is the correct size and shape. If the riser is too large, some Sugru can be removed with a sharp blade and sanded with fine sandpaper. If the riser is too small, more Sugru can be added since this material will bond with itself. By continuing this process, saxophonists will have a custom-made palm key riser that perfectly fits their hand.

Sugru Custom-Made Palm Key Risers. *Courtesy of Sugru.com*

SECRET 8: SELECTING A SAXOPHONE NECK STRAP

The saxophone neck strap is often overlooked when considering the essential components necessary for successful saxophone playing. However, the type of neck strap used is very important since it has a significant effect on the saxophonist's comfort level when practicing and performing and on instrument security. The more comfortable saxophonists are when practicing, the more likely they are to have longer practice sessions, improving musical skills at a faster pace.

There are many types of neck straps being manufactured in a variety of different styles, colors, and materials. When choosing a neck strap, saxophonists should carefully consider the strap design, comfort level, strap adjustment, and security before a selection is made.

Types of Neck Strap Designs

One type of neck strap design is the harness strap. This design is usually used for larger saxophones such as the baritone but may also be used for smaller instruments especially if the saxophonist is small in stature or if the instrument is to be carried for long distances, such as when marching in a parade. The harness strap works much like a backpack strap since it loops over the shoulders and around the back and snaps together in the front. This design allows the weight of the instrument to be evenly spread over a large portion of the body and puts no pressure on the neck. However, many saxophonists feel that this type of neck strap, while having an excellent design, is not necessary for smaller instruments because of their minimal weight and choose a neck strap that is smaller and less obtrusive to wear.

Neotech Soft Harness Strap. *Courtesy of Optechusa.com*

Another type of neck strap is a sling design. This type of strap loops over the left shoulder, around the back, and under the right arm and snaps together in the front. It is used for medium-sized saxophones such as the tenor and places the weight of the instrument on the left shoulder instead of the neck. Even though this strap has an excellent design, many saxophonists also choose not to wear it because they feel the weight of the tenor can be handled using a traditional strap that is held solely by the neck.

Neotech Sling Strap. *Courtesy of Optechusa.com*

A third type of neck strap is the traditional design in which the strap loops around the neck much like a necktie and attaches to the saxophone in the center of the body. The neck supports the entire weight of the saxophone in this design, and it is the one preferred most by saxophonists.

Other Considerations

Other aspects to be considered, in addition to the strap design, are comfort level, strap adjustment, and instrument security. With a traditional strap, the neck supports the entire weight of the instrument, which may be uncomfortable to wear for extended periods, especially if the part of the strap that touches the neck is slim and unpadded.

Also after playing with a slim, unpadded strap, some saxophonists begin to experience neck pain and tingling in the fingers of both hands. If these problems are not corrected, the saxophonist will not enjoy practicing nearly as much, which could result in reduced practice time and lack of progress.

One solution to these problems is to place a soft, thick cloth between the neck strap and the back of the neck to provide additional padding. Also wearing a shirt with a collar, which is placed between the strap and the back of the neck, will assist in relieving these symptoms. However, a better solution would be to purchase a more comfortable neck strap that has a wide, thick pad in the area that contacts the neck. There are several traditional neck straps designed with padding that is soft, flexible, shock absorbent, and durable, allowing the saxophonist to practice in comfort.

Another important factor to consider is the strap adjustment mechanism used for positioning the height of the saxophone. A neck strap should be designed in a way that allows for easy adjustment, preferably with just one hand, since the other hand will most likely be holding the saxophone. Once properly adjusted, the strap should also be stable and not move unexpectedly.

Instrument security, which is how securely the neck strap holds the saxophone, should also not be ignored. A neck strap should be designed with a hook that does not damage the saxophone but also holds the instrument securely so it does not accidentally come unhooked and fall to the ground. Some neck straps have an open hook that is made of a hard metal, such as steel, which can damage the saxophone and is also unsafe. These problems can both be solved by purchasing a strap with a strong nylon snap hook that will not damage the saxophone and is also safe since the hook completely encircles the saxophone ring, making it impossible to accidentally slip off.

Popular Neck Strap Brands

Neotech, BG, Protec, and Oleg are some neck strap brands that are very popular with saxophonists because they provide comfort, ease of adjustment, durability, and instrument security. When selecting a neck strap, it is important to narrow down the choices by examining how each strap addresses the factors stated above. After the choices have been narrowed down, it is recommended that the remaining neck straps be test-played to find the one that best fits the individual's needs.

Neotech Soft Strap. *Courtesy of Optechusa.com*

CHAPTER 2

Reed Strategies

SECRET 9: SELECTING REEDS

Proper reed selection is very important because the reed affects almost every aspect of playing, especially tone, intonation, response, range, embouchure formation, and endurance. There are many brands of reeds being produced from cane grown in various country regions. Since there are so many reed brands to choose from, it is necessary for saxophonists to narrow down the choices by getting recommendations from saxophone teachers, professional performers, and peers.

After this is done, saxophonists should test-play samples of the remaining reed brands to determine which one best suits their playing style. Factors such as reed strength, reed cut, type of cane, and the quality of the reed will determine how well a reed performs and should be carefully considered when making a reed selection.

Reed Brands

There are many reed manufacturers currently marketing saxophone reeds. However, two major companies, Rico and Vandoren, offer the most variety. Rico currently produces the following reeds: Rico, Rico Reserve Classic, Hemke, Grand Concert Select, Rico Plasticover, Rico Royal, Rico Jazz Select, and La Voz. Most of Rico's reeds are designed for both classical and jazz performance, but two of their reed cuts, Rico Jazz Select and La Voz, are designed especially for jazz and commercial performance.

Vandoren also produces a variety of saxophone reeds including Vandoren Traditional, V12, V16, Java, Java Filed Red Cut, and ZZ. While Traditional and V12 reeds are designed for both classical and jazz playing, jazz and commercial saxophonists mainly use Java, Java Filed Red Cut, V16, and ZZ reeds.

It is difficult to designate a reed as either for classical or jazz performance since the mouthpiece used and the saxophonist's playing style also greatly affect the overall tone. However, classical saxophone tone requires a reed and mouthpiece combination that produces a dark, mellow sound with little or no edge, and in general, jazz saxophone tone requires a reed and mouthpiece combination that produces a brighter sound with more edge. It is recommended that saxophonists try a variety of reed brands and cuts, both classical and jazz, to see which one works best for their particular performance situation.

Reed Strength

Reed strength refers to how hard or soft the reed is and usually correlates with the thickness. Reeds are numbered from 1 through 5, and as the number increases, so does the hardness or thickness of the reed. Most reed brands have strengths that increase in one-half number increments while a few increase in one-fourth increments. However, this numbering system is not standardized and reed strength may vary from one brand to another.

Factors used to determine the correct reed strength are the type of mouthpiece, mouthpiece facing, and tip opening and the performer's embouchure strength, breath support, and playing style. Saxophonists who use the correct reed strength will have a better chance of playing comfortably in tune and with a good tone.

Increasing Reed Strength

Beginning saxophonists usually start with softer reeds due to a weak embouchure, but as their embouchure strength and breath support develop, harder reeds are used. When increasing reed strength, saxophonists should gradually move up in one-half number reed strength sizes instead of whole numbers, which allows the embouchure time to adjust. For example, a saxophonist playing on a number 2 reed should move up to 2.5 before going to a number 3.

By increasing reed strength, tone quality, intonation, range, dynamic contrast, and other factors are improved. However, the process of increasing reed strength has led many saxophonists to believe that the harder the reed strength used, the better the performer. This myth is not true and saxophonists should be cautious when moving up to harder reeds. Saxophonists who play reeds that are too hard will have an airy, unfocused tone; instrument response problems; and premature embouchure fatigue.

On the other hand, reeds that are too soft will cause poor tone quality, response problems especially in the upper register, and intonation problems with the pitch going flat. This in turn may affect the embouchure, as the saxophonist will attempt to put too much embouchure pressure on the mouthpiece in order to pull the tone up to the correct pitch.

A guide to assist saxophonists in reed selection is the larger the tip opening of the mouthpiece, the smaller the reed strength number. Therefore mouthpieces with smaller tip openings will require a higher reed strength number. It is important for saxophonists to choose the correct reed strength as this will produce a full tone, create good instrument response, promote good intonation, and also alleviate premature embouchure fatigue.

Filed and Unfiled Reeds

Another aspect to consider when selecting a reed is the cut, either filed or unfiled. A filed reed, sometimes referred to as "double cut," has a thin layer of additional bark removed just below the vamp area, allowing the bark to form a straight line. This additional cut allows the reed to vibrate more freely, producing a brighter sound with better response.

Filed Reed

An unfiled reed, sometimes referred to as a "single cut," does not have the additional cut; the bark forms a U shape in the area below the vamp. This cut produces a darker tone with more resistance, as the reed is not as free to vibrate. Saxophonists should test-play both filed and unfiled reeds to see which cut works better with their particular mouthpiece and playing style.

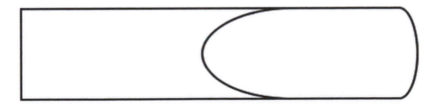

Unfiled Reed

Synthetic Reeds

In addition to cane reeds, some reed manufacturers also produce reeds that are made from synthetic materials. Legere, Forestone, Fibracell, and Bari are all manufacturers of synthetic saxophone reeds. The reeds are not affected by temperature and moisture changes and also last longer than conventional reeds. Synthetic reeds are made entirely from man-made materials and have no cane in them.

Although much more expensive than a traditional cane reed, these reeds will last a very long time. Synthetic reeds also do not have to be broken in nor do they have to be wet to play. In addition to being played under normal circumstances, doublers sometimes use these reeds in situations where they are required to pick up an instrument that has been idle for a while and play it instantly without having an opportunity to wet the reed.

Since these reeds are also more durable than conventional cane reeds, they are sometimes used for marching band and other outdoor performance events. However, synthetic reeds do not have the same feel as traditional cane when played and the tone is slightly different. For this reason, most saxophonists choose to play traditional cane reeds.

Purchasing Reeds

Once the reed brand, cut, and strength has been determined by playing samples of each reed, it is time to purchase reeds for use. When buying reeds, it is always best to purchase them by the box.

When reeds are made, they are mass-produced by machines that cut the reed based of the thickness of the cane and then package them in boxes of ten for soprano and alto saxophones and boxes of five for tenor and baritone saxophones. As a result of their mass production, there are several reeds out of each box that will not play well or at all. If purchasing only one or two reeds at a time, the saxophonist may receive the reeds out of a box that do not play. By purchasing the entire box of reeds, the performer is assured to get a selection of good reeds. Also, reeds are less expensive when purchased by the box, especially through online stores who sell mass quantities of reeds at close to wholesale prices.

If saxophonists decide to purchase only one or two reeds from a local music store, they should ask the salesclerk if they could select the reeds from the box rather than accepting what is handed to them. If saxophonists know what to look for when selecting a reed, they can pick the best reeds from the box while avoiding the reeds that do not play well.

When looking for the best reeds, saxophonists should examine the reeds by holding them up to a light. Good reeds will have a thick middle section called the heart, with the cane gradually tapering to the edge of the reed. The thickness of cane should be symmetrical on each side of the heart so the reed will be balanced. A balanced reed vibrates evenly on both sides because the cane is the same thickness.

Saxophonists should also look for a smooth vamp, which is the shaved portion of the reed. Vamps with coarse reed fibers may not perform well and may also be uncomfortable to the lower lip. By following these suggestions, saxophonists will increase their chances of purchasing playable reeds while avoiding the bad ones.

SECRET 10: BREAKING IN REEDS

The process of breaking in reeds is very important to the consistency, playability, and longevity of the reed. Breaking in a reed refers to the process of playing a new reed for short periods of time each day, gradually allowing the cane to acclimate to temperature, humidity, and the routine of getting wet and drying out. By completing the breaking-in process, the cane of the reed will not be damaged in the initial stages of playing, allowing the reed to perform better, play more consistently, and last longer.

The Breaking-In Process

The first step in the breaking-in process is to place the reeds in a bowl of lukewarm water for approximately four minutes to allow them time to soak in water. Saxophonists should make sure the entire reed is submerged in water, not just the tip.

Next the reed is removed from the water and placed on the mouthpiece. At this time, the reed should be played only for approximately three minutes at a medium soft dynamic level. Saxophonists should avoid playing in the extreme registers of the instrument or using any hard articulations.

After this, the reed is removed from the mouthpiece and placed in a reed case that contains a hard, flat surface for the reed to dry on. It is recommended that the reed case contain some type of humidity control system so the reed does not completely dry out.

Saxophonists should repeat this entire process for an additional four days, gradually increasing the amount of playing time each day by one minute. The dynamic level can also be increased up to a forte level while working toward the extreme ranges of the instrument, both low and high. After playing each day, the reed should be placed back into the reed storage device, allowing it to dry until the next day. After five days, the reed should be broken in and can be played normally.

SECRET 11: ADJUSTING REEDS

After completing the breaking-in process, there may be some reeds that do not play correctly. These reeds may be too hard, too soft, not balanced properly, or swollen and need to be adjusted. At this point, saxophonists who do not wish to work with reeds will throw them away. However, with a little work, most reeds can be adjusted, allowing them to be used for practice sessions and even performances. Since reeds are somewhat expensive, it is well worth the time and effort to learn how to adjust them.

Parts of the Reed

In order to properly adjust a reed, saxophonists must first learn the parts of a reed, which are illustrated in the diagram below. The tip of a reed is the thinnest part and comes into direct contact with the saxophonist's tongue when articulating. The tip is very delicate and should never be touched by the performer as it can be easily damaged. The vamp is the shaved portion of the reed that stretches from the tip to approximately halfway through the reed. The heart is located in the center of the vamp and is surrounded on both sides by the shoulders of the reed. The area below the vamp is not shaved and is covered with bark of the cane. The heel of the reed is the end opposite of the tip and is where the saxophonist can safely hold the reed without damaging it.

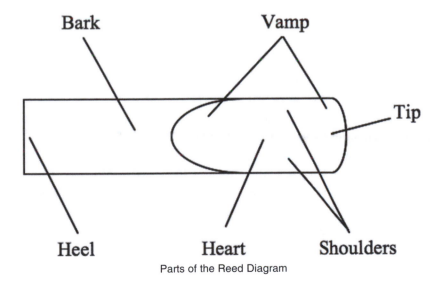

Parts of the Reed Diagram

Reed Adjustment

If a reed is too soft or too hard, adjustments may be made through either clipping or sanding the cane. Reeds that are too soft may be clipped using a reed clipper to make them harder. Reed clippers, which can be purchased at many music stores, work by removing the softer, thinner cane at the reed tip by clipping it off. This makes the reed tip thicker, resulting in a harder reed.

When clipping reeds, saxophonists should not remove too much of the tip at once since the removal of the smallest amount of cane will make a big difference in how the reed performs. After the reed has been clipped, it should be test-played to determine if any further work is necessary. If the reed is still too soft, an additional clipping may be necessary.

Reeds that are too hard may be sanded on their flat side with fine-grit sandpaper to make them softer. This process involves placing the sandpaper on a flat surface with the rough side facing up. The flat side of the reed is then slid back and forth against the sandpaper to remove small portions of cane over the entire flat surface of the reed. By removing cane, the reed is made thinner and softer.

When sanding a reed, saxophonists should only remove a small portion of cane at a time before test-playing since the removal of a little cane will greatly affect how the reed plays. Removing small amounts of cane throughout the reed will produce a softer, more playable reed.

Reeds that are not balanced properly will also need to be adjusted. In a balanced reed, both shoulders of the reed are the same thickness and vibrate evenly. If one shoulder of a reed is thicker than the other, they will vibrate at different frequencies, resulting in an unbalanced reed that performs poorly.

There are several ways to determine if a reed is properly balanced. The first is to play the reed by twisting the mouthpiece at an angle that allows only one side of the reed to touch the bottom lip. This side of the reed will be muted, allowing only the other side to vibrate. When doing this, the saxophonist should listen carefully to the sound. Now the mouthpiece should be twisted in the opposite direction and played with the other side of the reed muted. The saxophonist should then compare the tone produced by the two playings. If the tone is different, one side of the reed is thicker than the other and the reed is unbalanced. The thicker side of the reed is the one that needs to be adjusted and can be identified since it will vibrate at slower speed than the thinner side.

Another way to see if a reed is unbalanced is to visually inspect it by holding it up to a bright light. The saxophonist should examine both sides of the reed by looking to see how much light shines through each side of the reed. If light shines through one side of the reed more than the other, the reed is unbalanced. The thicker side of the reed is the one that needs to be adjusted and can be identified because it will not allow as much light to pass through as the thinner side.

To correct an unbalanced reed, the thicker side of the reed needs to be sanded or shaved with a reed knife on the shoulder of the shaved side of the reed, called the vamp. After removing a small portion of cane only on the thicker side, the saxophonist should visually inspect the reed again and also test-play it. Repeated sanding or shaving and test-playing may be necessary to get the reed perfectly balanced.

Sometimes reeds will swell after being soaked in water or after being played for a period of time. The swelling occurs on the flat side of the reed and prevents the reed from lying flat against the mouthpiece table. As a result, the reed will not respond properly and needs to be adjusted. To solve this problem, the saxophonist should lightly sand or shave the reed in the swollen area to remove the excess cane. This will allow the reed to lie perfectly flat against the mouthpiece table, correcting any response problems.

SECRET 12: THE REED SEALING TEST

A reed that is not sealing properly with the mouthpiece will have an adverse effect on saxophone tone and response. The reed sealing test is a way to check the reed, reed alignment, and mouthpiece to make sure the reed is sealing properly. The reed sealing test checks for leaks in the reed itself and between the reed and mouthpiece.

To perform the test, only the reed, ligature, mouthpiece, and saxophone neck are needed. With these pieces assembled, the saxophonist should seal off the large end of the saxophone neck with the palm of the hand. Next, all of the air should be sucked out of the mouthpiece and neck at the other end, creating a vacuum. This action should cause the tip of the reed to close and stick to the mouthpiece for several seconds. After that time, the reed should pop back to its normal position, making an audible popping sound. If this happens, the reed is sealing properly with the mouthpiece.

If a vacuum cannot be created, the saxophonist should carefully examine the reed and mouthpiece because a leak has developed somewhere between the two. The first thing to be inspected is the reed. If the reed is split, swollen, or not properly aligned with the mouthpiece, the reed will not seal properly and should be discarded or adjusted.

If no problems are found with the reed, the mouthpiece should be examined for damage or to see if the table is warped. A way to check for a mouthpiece problem is to perform the reed sealing test with several other new reeds. If a vacuum cannot be established with any of these reeds, most likely the mouthpiece is damaged or warped and will need to be replaced.

SECRET 13: REED STORAGE

After a practice session or performance is finished, the saxophonist should remove the reed from the mouthpiece and properly store it in a reed case. If the reed is left on the mouthpiece or not stored properly, it may be accidentally damaged or warp as it dries out, which will cause response problems and also diminish the life of the reed. Reeds that are stored properly play more consistently, which improves performance and also gives the saxophonist the confidence of knowing that the reed will remain stable throughout a concert.

Reed Cases

There are several types of reed cases available for storing reeds that vary in price and features offered. In order to properly store reeds, a reed case must contain a secure method of holding the reeds in place and a hard, flat surface that will keep the reeds from warping as they dry. Most reed cases are designed to hold from four to eight reeds; are made from plastic, wood, or metal; and contain a glass or Plexiglas bed for the reeds to lie on.

An additional feature that some reed cases offer is a way to control the humidity so reeds do not dry out completely or too fast. This is usually accomplished by some type of disposable humidity pack that is placed in the reed case alongside the reeds. This pack usually lasts from one to two months before it has to be replaced.

If a reed case is purchased that does not contain a method for controlling humidity, one solution is to place the reed case into a Ziploc plastic bag along with a humidity pack. This will achieve the same result as if the pack was inside the case itself. La Voz, Protec, Rico, Selmer, and Vandoren currently manufacture reed cases that are used by many professional saxophonists and offer an excellent way to store reeds.

Rico Reed Case with Humidity Control Pack.
Courtesy of Ricoreeds.com

Making a Reed Case

Some saxophonists prefer to make their own reed cases, which is also a viable option. To construct a reed case, a plastic airtight container with a removable lid is needed. Next a small sheet of Plexiglas should be obtained and cut into plates that are the appropriate size to fit into the container. A hacksaw can be used to cut the Plexiglas sheet into the smaller plates. Large rubber bands are used to hold individual reeds flat to the Plexiglas plates by stretching them across the body of the reed and around the plate.

To control humidity, a small moist sponge can be placed in the container with the reeds. To control the growth of mold, a small amount of mouthwash can be applied to the sponge since the alcohol contained in the mouthwash will kill any mold before it can accumulate. No matter what method of reed storage is used, it is important for saxophonists to have a method of correctly storing reeds. Properly stored reeds will have enhanced performance and consistency and increased longevity, saving the saxophonist money and providing peace of mind.

SECRET 14: ROTATING REEDS

It is recommended that saxophonists rotate their reeds when practicing or performing instead of playing one reed until it is worn out and then replacing it with a new one. Rotating reeds provides several advantages, one of which is increasing the life span of the reed. By rotating reeds, the cane fibers of the reed are allowed to recover after each playing, which greatly extends the life of the reed.

Another advantage of rotating reeds is that the saxophonist will always have backup reeds in case something happens to the primary reed in use. Sometimes a reed that is reserved for a performance may not play well on the day of the event. This may be due to a change in altitude, humidity level, or temperature; concert hall conditions; damage to the reed; or simple wearing out. By rotating reeds, the saxophonist will always have a reed to play when the primary reed will not.

A third benefit from reed rotation is that there will be little or no embouchure adjustment needed when switching from one reed to the next. When saxophonists play one reed until it is worn out and then switch to a new one, there is a big difference between the two. The new reed will be much harder to blow, requiring adjustments to be made in embouchure and breath support. These last-minute adjustments may feel very uncomfortable to saxophonists not only physically but also mentally, shifting their focus from the music being performed to concerns about the reed. This usually affects the music performance in an adverse way.

When rotating reeds, the exact number of reeds included in the rotation is a personal choice. Some saxophonists may rotate seven reeds, one for each day of the week, while others prefer more or less. It is highly suggested that at least four reeds be included in the rotation, while other reeds are constantly being worked in to replace reeds that are worn.

In order to keep track of the reed rotation, a labeling system should be used where each reed receives a number reminding the saxophonist which reed is next in the rotation. For example, if the reeds are numbered 1 through 4 and the saxophonist is currently playing on reed number 3, the next reed in the rotation would be reed number 4, followed by reed number 1. The rotated reeds should also be properly stored in a reed case equipped with some type of humidity control system to keep them from being damaged or becoming warped.

In addition to the rotation number, the saxophonist may also want to place an additional label on each reed when preparing for an upcoming performance. The additional label ranks the reeds based on their playability. If the saxophonist is using numbers to label the reeds for rotation purposes, a lettering system could be used to rank the reeds for how well they play. The best reed could be labeled with the letter A, the second-best reed with a B, and so on.

This labeling system will be very helpful when selecting the best reeds to be used in an upcoming performance even though the rankings could change depending upon the performance venue and the climate. Also when preparing for an upcoming performance, some saxophonists may wish to remove the performance reeds from the normal rotation in order to save them for the concert. This decision is a personal choice and is perfectly acceptable.

SECRET 15: REVIVING DEAD REEDS

Every cane saxophone reed will sooner or later wear out due to damage, the cane becoming too soft, or the tone and response of the reed reaching such a poor level that the reed is unplayable. These reeds are referred to as being "dead" and are thrown away by most saxophonists when they reach this stage in their life. However, for saxophonists who are not ready to throw a dead reed away, there are ways to revive it, allowing some additional time to the reed's life.

Some saxophonists prolong the life of a dead reed that is too soft by clipping it, which is a viable option as long as the tone does not become too adversely affected. However, a clipped reed will feel and play differently due to the shape of the clipped tip, which is never exactly the same as the original reed, and a reed can only be clipped so many times before it is useless.

Some reeds are considered dead not because they are too soft but because the tone produced is not very good. This can be due to the cane fibers being damaged or clogged, and clipping the reed will not improve this condition.

A second way to revive a dead reed is to place it in warm water and gently scrub the cane with either the fingers or a soft cloth, making sure to not break the fibers. This action will unclog the cane, allowing the reed to vibrate more freely and increasing its resonance, response, and life span.

A third way to revive a dead reed is to place it in a bowl of hydrogen peroxide for several minutes. The hydrogen peroxide will bubble into the cane fibers, cleansing them of any impurities that may be clogging them up. When the reed is finished soaking, remove and rinse it with warm water before playing.

These suggestions for reed revival may be used separately or in combination with each other depending on what works best for each performer. Because a dead reed is unplayable in its current condition, saxophonists are encouraged to try these methods since they do not have to worry about further damaging the reed. The worst thing that could happen is that the condition of the reed is not improved.

CHAPTER 3

Embouchure Strategies

SECRET 16: FORMING A CORRECT EMBOUCHURE

Forming a correct embouchure is one of the most important aspects of playing the saxophone. Without a correct embouchure, a saxophonist's tone, intonation, response, musical expressiveness, and performance enjoyment will be severely hindered. In addition, it is extremely important to establish a correct embouchure in the very beginning stages of development since a poorly formed embouchure is difficult to change once it has been learned. Therefore, beginning saxophonists and their teachers should carefully monitor embouchure formation from the very first lesson, correcting any flaws until the formation of a correct embouchure becomes a habit.

However, if a saxophonist has a poor embouchure, it can be corrected with the right instruction, through careful monitoring and much patience. Perhaps the most important factor in improving a poor embouchure is the saxophonist's desire to change. If performers are not satisfied with their progress and have a sincere desire to improve, anything is possible.

The O Shape

To form a correct saxophone embouchure, the mouth and lips should form an O shape much as if saying the vowel O or as if to whistle. Saxophonists should form this position with the mouth and then slide the mouthpiece into the mouth while holding the O formation. Approximately one half inch of the mouthpiece should be taken into the mouth, which will position the lower teeth at the optimum position for reed control and response. The top teeth are placed on the top of the mouthpiece as the corners of the mouth contract around the sides. The mouthpiece when slid into the mouth will automatically pull the correct amount of lower lip over the teeth, which is usually about half of the red fleshy part.

As the saxophonist blows air into the mouthpiece using proper breath support, the correct amount of embouchure pressure should occur naturally as the facial muscles tighten to keep the air from leaking around the mouth. The saxophonist should hold the O position and not allow it to move when performing this step. This is perhaps the most difficult part of embouchure formation because as air pressure builds the natural tendency is to allow the O position to collapse.

Great care must be taken to ensure that the chin muscles located directly below the lower lip do not bunch up as air enters the mouthpiece. The chin muscles should be held flat against the chin in the position of saying O or whistling. The overall feeling is one of pushing the chin muscles down and away from the body. It may also feel like the skin over the chin muscles is being slightly stretched as the muscles are pushed down and away from the body.

Pressure from the lower teeth and jaw should be kept to a minimum since this restricts reed vibration, causes intonation problems, and can also cause a sore lower lip. When first performing this procedure, only the mouthpiece and neck of the instrument should be used, allowing the performer to concentrate only on embouchure formation and not instrument position. As the saxophonist feels more comfortable with this procedure, the instrument may be added.

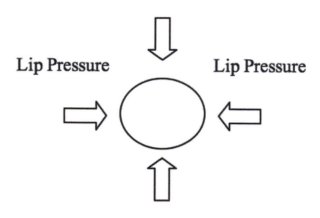

The O Embouchure Position
Equal Lip Pressure around the Mouthpiece with Chin
Muscles Pushing Down

Using a Mirror

Saxophonists should use a mirror to examine the chin muscles when initially forming the embouchure because it may be difficult to feel if the chin muscles are in the proper position. A small car visor mirror is a perfect choice for this task. Performers can carry the mirror in their case and place it on the music stand when practicing in order to check their embouchure. This may be necessary for several days or longer until proper embouchure formation becomes natural.

In the beginning, saxophonists may form the correct embouchure, but as they begin to focus on other aspects of playing, the embouchure may slip back into its old position undetected. Constant examination through the use of a mirror will keep this from happening. After a short period of time, correct embouchure formation will become a natural occurrence and use of a mirror can be halted.

SECRET 17: DETERMINING PROPER EMBOUCHURE PRESSURE

Playing with the correct amount of embouchure pressure is a very important aspect of saxophone performance since too much or too little pressure will have an adverse effect on tone production, intonation, and response. Saxophonists that play with too much embouchure pressure usually have a small, pinched tone; intonation that is sharp especially in the upper register; poor response in the low register; problems with producing vibrato; and a sore lower lip. It is essential that saxophonists check their embouchure pressure to determine if the proper amount is being used and make corrections if necessary.

There are two primary methods saxophonists use to check for correct embouchure pressure. The first method is to start a tone using only the mouthpiece and neck of the instrument. There are two pitches that can be produced depending on how much pressure is applied to the mouthpiece. The embouchure pressure used by most classical performers produces a Concert A♭ with the mouthpiece positioned on the neck where it is normally placed when the saxophone is in tune. However, some jazz saxophonists play with less embouchure pressure, producing a Concert G.

Concert A♭: Classical and Concert G: Jazz

Many times saxophonists will produce a pitch higher than the Concert A♭, indicating that too much pressure is being applied to the mouthpiece. If this is the case, the performer should reduce the amount of pressure applied by the lower lip, jaw, and teeth while keeping the air pressure constant in the oral cavity. It is important to drop the lower jaw, reducing embouchure pressure without reducing the air pressure inside the mouth. Simply blowing more softly is not the answer. The air pressure inside the mouth should not change.

A second method used to check correct embouchure pressure is for the saxophonist to play octaves slurring from the lower octave to the upper and then back down. An excellent note to use for this exercise is low A, on the second space of the staff. The saxophonist should play a low A and then slur up to the A located an octave higher by pressing the octave key. No change in air or embouchure pressure should take place when doing this. After the upper A sounds, the saxophonist should release the octave key and the lower A should sound immediately. If the low A does not sound immediately or is delayed, embouchure pressure is too great and should be reduced by dropping the jaw while keeping the air pressure constant. When the jaw pressure is reduced and the low A sounds, the correct embouchure pressure for performing both notes has been established.

If jaw pressure is reduced and the low A still does not sound, the saxophonist should take a little more mouthpiece into the mouth. This should allow the reed to vibrate more freely, improving tonal resonance and response. With correct embouchure pressure, the performer should be able to slur octaves in 16th notes with ease, assuming the instrument and reed are in proper playing condition. This exercise can also be performed on a variety of other notes that use only the octave key to change registers.

Embouchure Pressure Exercise

It is important for saxophonists to remember that the change in octaves is due only to the octave key being pressed and not due to a change in pressure. It is also very important for saxophonists not to move their embouchure when playing in different registers of the instrument. Some performers develop a bad habit of involuntarily moving the lower jaw especially when playing in the low register. This movement should be avoided as it causes notes to have different timbres and may also cause intonation and response problems.

Another variation of this exercise is to allow another person to quickly depress and release the octave key while the saxophonist is holding the note. By doing this, the embouchure cannot be adjusted for each note since the performer does not know when the octave key will be depressed and released. This is an excellent exercise for stopping involuntary movement of the embouchure.

One consistent embouchure setting should be used to play the entire range of the instrument. This setting can be found by playing the lowest note on the saxophone, the low B♭. The saxophonist should play low B♭ and note the amount of embouchure pressure used and the mouthpiece placement. This setting should then be maintained as the saxophonist plays in all other registers.

Embouchure Fatigue

When initially correcting poor embouchure formation, fatigue of the embouchure muscles may be experienced after playing for only a short while. However, endurance will develop quickly and the saxophonist will be able to play for much longer periods of time. If the embouchure collapses due to fatigue, practice should stop immediately. This will ensure that the performer does not begin to bite into the lower lip due to a lack of embouchure muscle support or revert back to the old incorrect embouchure formation. After a short period of rest, the embouchure muscles will regain their strength and practice may resume.

SECRET 18: DETERMINING PROPER MOUTHPIECE PLACEMENT

Proper mouthpiece placement and mouthpiece angle have a huge effect on saxophone tone and response. The exact placement of the mouthpiece varies depending on the facial features of the performer and the type of mouthpiece facing used.

Mouthpiece angle can also vary especially when switching from one saxophone type to another, such as alto to tenor. Since every saxophonist is a unique individual, each performer learns the exact mouthpiece placement and angle through experimentation and trial and error. However, there are some general guidelines that all saxophonists should follow to get them headed in the right direction.

Mouthpiece Placement

When the correct amount of mouthpiece is placed in the mouth, a saxophonist's lower teeth will be in line with the point at which the reed and mouthpiece separate. This is equal to taking about one half inch of mouthpiece into the mouth. To find the exact point, the performer can carefully slip a sheet of paper in between the reed and mouthpiece and slide it down until it first meets resistance. This resistance identifies the point where the reed and mouthpiece separate and is the fulcrum for optimum control. The saxophonist can mark this point on the reed and then make sure to take enough mouthpiece in the mouth to allow the lower teeth to be in line with this point.

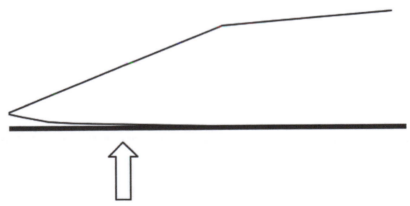

Alignment of Lower Teeth with Mouthpiece and Reed

The performer should also experiment with taking slightly differing amounts of mouthpiece in the mouth while listening for optimum tone and control. If not enough mouthpiece is taken into the mouth, a small, muted tone and poor instrument response will be the result. If too much mouthpiece is taken, the tone will become harsh and uncontrolled.

If saxophonists are having problems with note response especially when slur-ring quickly from one register to the next and they are sure their embouchure pressure is correct, taking a little more mouthpiece into the mouth should solve the problem. Sometimes performers with response problems do not have enough mouthpiece in the mouth to allow the instrument to work properly.

Mouthpiece Angle

Mouthpiece angle is also a factor in tone production and instrument response. The proper mouthpiece angle slightly varies depending on the type of saxophone being played and the playing style of the performer. The mouthpiece angle for soprano and alto saxophones is slightly downward. When playing the tenor and baritone saxophones, the mouthpiece is angled less, almost going straight in the mouth.

As a mouthpiece is angled more into the body, the lip pressure moves forward from directly on top of the lower teeth to a position more on the front of the teeth. This movement will have an effect on the tone and response of the instrument. There is some latitude in the exact mouthpiece angle to be used as many perform-ers angle their instruments in a way that assists them in achieving a desired tone quality. Perhaps the best way for saxophonists to determine the correct mouth-piece angle is to try different positions while listening to the tone. When the tone is at its optimum resonance, the correct angle has been established.

SECRET 19: CAUSES OF A SORE LIP

Saxophonists who have a rigorous practice schedule sometimes complain of a sore or sensitive lower lip. As a result, they may have to reduce their practice time or stop practicing altogether to allow the lip time to heal. If performers choose to practice with a sore lip due to an impending performance, frustration may occur due to the pain experienced while practicing or to impeded progress.

Soreness may occur in two different areas of the lower lip: the dry, outside portion that touches the reed when playing or the inside, wet portion that touches the lower teeth when playing. It is of extreme importance to determine the cause of lower lip soreness so that a remedy can be put into effect to alleviate the problem.

Soreness of the Outside Lower Lip

If soreness occurs on the top outside area of the lower lip, this is due to contact with the vibrating reed. The outside portion of the lower lip may become sore and actually begin to bleed due to contact with the reed if the saxophonist has an extensive practice schedule. If the performer is experiencing lip soreness in this outer area of the lower lip, patience is the answer. This type of soreness is usually associated with beginning-level performers or with performers who have just started a more rigorous practice schedule.

To solve this problem, saxophonists should gradually increase their practice time, allowing the lower lip time to adjust to longer contact to the vibrating reed. If the lip becomes sore or begins to bleed, practice should be halted to allow the lip time to heal.

The type of reed used may also be a factor in soreness of the outer lower lip. Reeds made entirely of synthetic materials or cane reeds that are plastic coated for longer life may cause the lower lip to become sore more quickly than regular cane reeds. Also reeds that have coarse cane fibers on the vamp may irritate the lower lip more than a reed that has a smoother finish. However, this coarseness can be easily corrected by lightly sanding the rough area using fine-grade sandpaper until it is smooth.

In addition, the lower lip may become sore by practicing on a narrow metal mouthpiece, in which the reed is slightly wider than the mouthpiece rails. Since the reed is wider than the mouthpiece, the reed sides may cut into the lower lip, causing bleeding and soreness. If this is the case, the sides of the reed can be lightly sanded, making it narrower and alleviating the problem.

To adjust a reed that is too wide for the mouthpiece, the saxophonist should first make a mark on the two edges of the reed with a pencil. Then using fine-grit sandpaper, sand each side of the reed just enough to remove the pencil mark, only about two or three strokes on each side. When sanding, place the sandpaper on a flat surface and sand the reed by lightly pushing the reed against the sandpaper in one direction. When the pencil line is gone, the reed should be the correct width. By performing this procedure on the sides of the reed, the lower lip will avoid being cut and, as an added benefit, reed response will be increased. No matter what the exact cause of soreness is, over a short period of time the outer area of the lower lip will toughen up, allowing the saxophonist to practice for extended periods without developing a sore lip.

Soreness of the Inside Lower Lip

If the lower lip is sore on the inside, smooth portion just above the lower teeth, the cause is due to pressure from the lower teeth. Even if this pressure is minimal, soreness may still occur as small indentions are made on the underside of the lower lip by contact from the lower teeth. This soreness can be very frustrating to the saxophonist due to the pain experienced when practicing, a loss of practice time as the lip is allowed to heal, impeded progress, and the lack of pure enjoyment when practicing and performing. In addition, if a chronic sore lip is severe and allowed to continue over a long period of time, permanent damage to the nerves of the lower lip may result.

Several factors that directly influence the amount of pressure exerted on the lower lip are breath support, embouchure formation, mouthpiece and reed selection, sharpness of lower teeth, and braces. If a saxophonist is experiencing soreness and pain in this area of the lower lip, each of the five above factors should be examined first to determine if the cause of lower lip pain can be eliminated through adjustment in one of these areas.

Breath support is a very important aspect with regard to embouchure pressure. If performers do not provide enough breath support when playing, an excessive amount of jaw pressure might be used to compensate for the difference, resulting in teeth marks on the lower lip. When playing, saxophonists should breathe using the diaphragm, pushing a consistent, fast-moving, concentrated flow of air to the mouthpiece. If this is done, any excessive pressure applied to the lower lip from the teeth will be eliminated.

Incorrect embouchure formation can also cause a sore lower lip due to inadequate support from the facial muscles located underneath the bottom lip. The most common embouchure problem is the collapse and bunching up of chin muscles under the lower lip. When the chin muscles are allowed to bunch up, too much lower lip comes into contact with the reed, creating tone and response problems. In addition, the support needed to suspend the lower lip over the bottom teeth is absent, which can result in teeth marks on the underside of the lip. Students who try to perform with an incorrect embouchure may experience poor tone, intonation problems, poor instrument response, and many times a chronic sore lower lip.

Another cause of a sore lip could be incorrect mouthpiece and reed selection. If a mouthpiece and reed combination require more embouchure strength than a saxophonist can give, the result will be excessive jaw pressure and teeth marks on the lower lip. To solve this problem, saxophonists should select a mouthpiece and reed that can be easily controlled and gradually move into larger mouthpiece tip openings or harder reeds.

The sharpness of the lower teeth has a direct effect on lower lip soreness and pain. In some saxophonists, even when using correct breath support, correct embouchure formation, and the appropriate mouthpiece and reed, teeth marks can still occur on the lower lip, especially if the lower teeth are sharp. Lower teeth can be very sharp in saxophonists who have an overbite in which the top teeth and lower teeth never touch at their tips. As a result, the lower teeth can remain very sharp because the chewing motion never dulls the tips. To solve this problem, some saxophonists elect to have their lower teeth filed by a dentist to make playing more comfortable. However, the dentist can only file so much off the teeth to dull them and many times this is not enough to alleviate the problem.

Braces are also a major factor in lower lip soreness and pain. Many people must wear braces during their formative years of development, usually beginning in middle school and junior high school. This is also the same time that many musicians begin playing the saxophone. In addition to lower lip pain caused by contact with the lower teeth, braces can be a major source of frustration if they irritate the lower lip. Some dentists recommend the use of wax on the braces to alleviate this problem, but many times this is not effective. If this is the case, saxophonists must cope with this situation until the braces are removed.

SECRET 20: MAKING A TEMPORARY COVER FOR THE LOWER TEETH

Some saxophonists develop a chronic sore lip even though embouchure, breath support, and other factors regarding performance are being performed correctly. Many of these saxophonists learn to cope with this issue by developing a tougher lower lip or by slightly adjusting the placement of the lower lip so the teeth contact a different spot of the lip each time they perform. For others, a different solution is needed. An excellent choice for those performers is to use a cover for the lower teeth.

What Is a Cover?

The term *cover* refers to a dental device placed over the lower teeth that provides a cushion between the teeth and lower lip as the saxophone embouchure is formed. A cover creates a smooth contact point for the lower lip and teeth and eliminates teeth abrasions sometimes made on the lip even when the embouchure is formed correctly. By providing a more comfortable contact point for the lower lip and teeth, the cover increases practice productivity, lengthens practice time, and, most of all, allows the student to practice and perform without experiencing any pain in the lower lip.

Types of Covers

Covers can be made by individual performers or by their dentist or be bought from a music store. Advantages of individuals making their own covers are they are much less expensive, they can be more conveniently adjusted to fit the saxophonist's specific needs, and if the cover is lost, the performer can quickly replace it.

Covers can be made out of a variety of materials depending on the saxophonist's preferences and can be temporary or more permanent. Some performers simply fold a piece of paper or plastic over the lower teeth to reduce lower lip pain. However, this method is not recommended because paper or plastic is not a stable material and will last for only a short period of time.

Another problem with this method is the shape of the paper or plastic is not consistent from one practice session to another. The paper or plastic may not be folded exactly the same way from one practice session to another, and these materials may not actually take the shape of the teeth as they are folded over them. This may allow for the cover to move during a performance and also makes it impossible for the cover to be placed on the lower teeth in a consistent manner. In addition, these materials will begin to deteriorate immediately after they are placed in the mouth. Therefore, the saxophonist is playing with a slightly different embouchure each practice session due to a lack of consistency.

Making a Wax/Fiber Cover for the Lower Teeth

A better choice for making covers is a wax and fiber material found in denture pads. Denture pads are designed to provide a snug fit between the gum and dentures. The wax and fiber material found in denture pads is flexible, will mold to the teeth, and is stable enough to make excellent covers. EZO is a very common brand of denture pads and can be purchased inexpensively at many department stores or drugstores. They usually are sold with fifteen pads in a box and are made in different shapes (for upper or lower dentures) and thicknesses (light, medium, or heavy gauges). Lower heavy gauge is recommended.

EZO Denture Cushions

The following is a step-by-step procedure for making a cover from an EZO denture pad.

1. Take one denture pad and cut it into the approximate size and shape to cover the bottom four front teeth. Usually a small rectangle shape with rounded corners works best. (One denture pad will make between five and seven covers depending upon their size.)

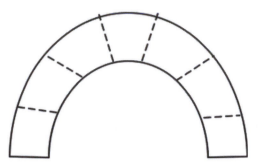

Pattern for Cutting EZO Denture Cushions

2. Fold the cover over the bottom teeth and gently press down and inward toward the teeth, allowing the cover to conform. As the cover becomes warm from being placed in the mouth, it will become more flexible and take on the shape and size of the teeth. (Make sure that the cover does not extend too far down on the teeth where it may touch and irritate the gums.)

3. Once the cover is molded to the lower teeth, the saxophonist should play the instrument while adjusting the cover as it settles in. The cover may move slightly and may need to be centered again over the lower teeth. As playing continues, the tips of the lower teeth will make indentions into the wax, which will keep the cover from moving.

4. The cover, when removed from the mouth, will harden into the shape of the lower teeth. This will allow the saxophonist at the next practice session to simply slip the cover over the teeth for a perfect fit. Although the cover when placed back into the mouth will become flexible again, if placed over the teeth, it will not lose its shape.

5. As the saxophonist practices with the cover for only a short period of time, the cover will feel like a natural part of the embouchure.

Covers made from denture pads are easy to make and will last for several weeks to several months depending on the amount of practice and the amount of lower jaw pressure applied by the saxophonist when playing. Eventually, the lower teeth will wear through the cover and another one will have to be made. However, one box of denture pads could last several years.

SECRET 21: MAKING A PERMANENT COVER FOR THE LOWER TEETH

Covers may be made from another more permanent material taken from youth athletic mouth guards (like those used by football performers to protect the teeth). This material, although permanent, is more difficult to work with than the wax and fiber denture pads and should only be used after the saxophonist has become accustomed to making and playing covers made from other materials.

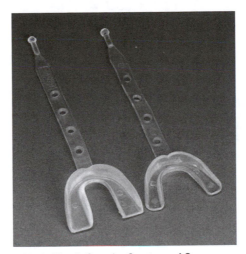

Athletic Mouth Guards. *Courtesy of Ssww.com*

The following is a step-by-step procedure for making a cover from youth athletic mouth guards.

1. Purchase a youth athletic mouth guard found in many sports and department stores. (Adult mouth guards are too thick and should not be used.) These mouth guards come in two colors: transparent and black. A transparent color may be preferred because it cannot be seen in the mouth.
2. The mouth guard should be cut into the appropriate size to cover the bottom four front teeth. A small rectangle shape with rounded corners is recommended. Although different parts of the mouth guard may be used, the center section is preferred and not the sides of the mouth guard due to their variation in thickness. However, the strap that is designed to hold the mouth guard to the football helmet may also be used.

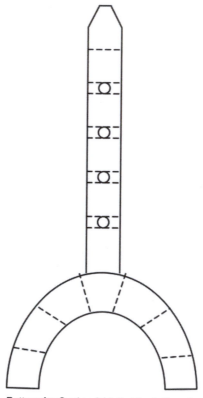

Pattern for Cutting Athletic Mouth Guards

3. The cover should now be placed on a microwave-safe plate or on a paper towel and heated in a microwave. The microwave setting should be on "high" and the cover should be heated for approximately three minutes.

4. After the cover is heated, it should carefully be removed from the plate or paper towel. The temperature of the cover can be checked by lightly touching the cover with a finger before picking it up. Care should be taken so the cover does not burn the skin. If the cover is too hot to be picked up, it should be allowed to cool but not for too long. The material needs to remain flexible so it can be molded to the teeth.

5. After the cover is cool enough to be picked up, it should be placed over the bottom four front teeth and gently pressed around the teeth. The cover will instantly conform to the teeth as it continues to cool. (Make sure that the cover does not extend too far down on the teeth where it may touch and irritate the gums.)

6. This process of heating and molding the cover may take several attempts before a perfect fit is achieved. After several attempts, however, a very comfortable, well-fitted cover can be attained. These covers, although more

difficult to make, will last indefinitely. If for some reason the lower teeth do eventually cut through the cover, the cover can be reheated in the microwave and molded to the teeth again.

Using a Cover

When playing with a cover for the first time, the saxophonist must be patient, allowing the embouchure to adjust to the additional cushion that is now over the lower teeth. The performers may feel uncomfortable with using a cover initially, but after a short period of adjustment, they will be able to perform as they have always done but with the added comfort of a cover. Saxophonists will also notice that they can practice for longer periods of time without injury to the lower lip.

Although the use of a cover can provide for more comfortable practice sessions and lengthen practice time, it should not be used as a remedy for incorrect breath support, embouchure, or mouthpiece and reed selection. Covers should only be used after a correct and stable embouchure has been established and proper selection of mouthpiece and reeds has been made. The decision to use or not to use a cover is a choice that each individual saxophonist must make. For saxophonists who have a chronic sore lower lip, covers can provide a solution and return the joy to performing once again.

CHAPTER 4

Tone Strategies

SECRET 22: BREATHING EXERCISES

Proper breath support is one of the most important aspects of playing a wind instrument. However, some saxophonists ignore this aspect of performance since other factors occurring simultaneously also require their attention. If saxophonists do not play with the proper breath support, numerous performance problems are likely to result. To avoid these problems, diaphragmic breathing should be used to establish proper breath support, allowing the embouchure and instrument to correctly work together. Although the method is sometimes not an instinctual habit for many players, with focused practice, this method of breathing can be mastered and will greatly enhance a saxophonist's performance ability.

Inhalation

The first factor in developing breath support is proper air intake. The saxophonist should breathe air in through the corners of the mouth while keeping the rest of the embouchure in place on the mouthpiece. An alternative to this method is to drop the lower jaw, keeping the lower lip in place over the lower teeth, and breathe in through the center of the mouth. Either method is acceptable and should be determined by the individual performer. When breathing in, air should be inhaled quickly and deeply in one large breath. As the diaphragm drops downward, it forces the waist area to expand outward in all directions, even on the sides and back. The shoulders should not rise but remain motionless. Saxophonists should think of filling up the body with air, starting with the area around the belt buckle and moving up to the head. Imagine pouring water into a container filling it up from the bottom.

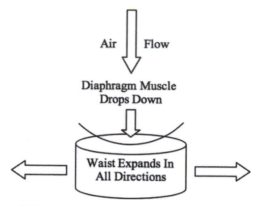

Airflow Downward into Lungs during Inhalation

Exhalation

When breathing out, the saxophonist should push the air upward with the diaphragm muscle located in the area just below the rib cage. The visible effect will be the waist area contracting to its original position before the breath was taken. This motion is much more intense than breathing out normally. When blowing air into the instrument, a narrow, steady stream of pressurized air should be blown throughout the duration of the phrase being played.

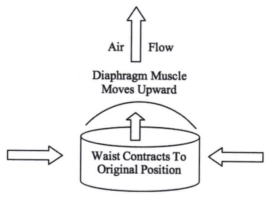

Airflow Upward and Out of Lungs during Exhalation

Air Pressure

When correctly performing the breathing motion, correct air pressure will be maintained in the oral cavity, allowing the embouchure to work properly. In addition, by having air pressure pushing outward in all directions in the oral cavity, the saxophone can be played with less embouchure pressure from the lower jaw and teeth on the lower lip. Air pressure pushing downward on the jaw and lower teeth from inside the oral cavity helps equalize the upward pressure applied from the jaw and lower teeth. This will allow the reed to vibrate more freely, producing a more resonant sound.

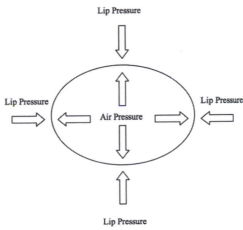

Embouchure Air Pressure

Breathing Exercises

One exercise to practice proper breathing is for the saxophonist to lie down on the back or stand with the back against a wall while placing a hand on the stomach. Next a large breath should be taken through the mouth making sure that the waist expands in all directions as air enters the body. When performed properly, it will feel as if the air is filling up the body starting at the belt buckle and moving up to the head. The shoulders should not move during this process. If they do, the process is being performed incorrectly and must be tried again. Lying down or standing with the back against a wall should assist in this matter by holding the shoulders stationary while inhalation is taking place.

Another alternative position for this exercise in addition to lying down or standing with the back against a wall is to sit in a chair and bend over, placing the chest against the knees. This position will also assist in keeping the shoulders stationary during inhalation.

When exhaling, the saxophonist should blow a narrow, consistent stream of pressurized air in a slow, controlled manner with the diaphragm muscle. As a result, the waist area that was expanded during inhalation will return to its original position. When exhaling, the lips should be shaped in an O position, which will continue to focus the air into a narrow, concentrated stream similar to one used to blow out a candle. This will approximate the motion performed when actually playing the instrument. The saxophonist should practice this exercise by inhaling for two seconds and exhaling for eight seconds. With practice, a performer will develop the ability to inhale a large quantity of air in one quick breath, allowing long phrases to be played with no loss in tone quality or control.

The following is a review of proper breathing procedures:

1. Breathe in quickly and deeply through the mouth.
2. Fill up the body with air from the bottom up.
3. The waist should expand outward while the shoulders remain motionless.
4. Breathe out by pushing the air upward with the diaphragm.
5. A narrow, consistent, controlled stream of air should be blown out.
6. The waist should contract back to its original position.
7. Proper air pressure should be maintained in the oral cavity.
8. With proper air pressure, less jaw and lower teeth pressure is needed.

SECRET 23: FINDING THE OPTIMUM TONGUE POSITION

A saxophonist's tongue position has a direct effect on tone, response, and the ability to articulate quickly. The best tongue position is one that is comfortable, produces a good tone, provides a quick response in all registers, and places the tip of the tongue close to the reed for quick and clean articulation. It is very important for saxophonists to find this position since without it progress will be impeded.

The best tongue position is one that is high in the oral cavity where the back of the tongue is close to roof of the mouth. In this position, the sides of the tongue touch the sides of the upper teeth as if saying the word *he* or *her*. By using a high tongue position, the oral cavity is made smaller, keeping the airstream narrow, focused, and quickly moving. In addition to assisting in good tone production, response, and articulation, this position will also assist the saxophonist in playing overtones and the altissimo register. Although this tongue position may change slightly when playing in different registers, the overall position should basically stay the same. By using this position, saxophonists will discover that their tone is more focused, response is better, articulation is quicker, and overall, playing the instrument is easier.

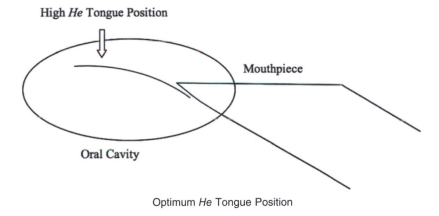

Optimum *He* Tongue Position

SECRET 24: PLAYING WITH AN OPEN THROAT

The term *open throat* means that the throat is relaxed and unrestricted, allowing the airstream to flow easily from the lungs into the oral cavity. Playing with an open throat will greatly assist the saxophonist in producing good tone, intonation, and response. It is sometimes difficult for saxophonists to know if they are playing with an open throat because the inside of the throat cannot be observed when performing. However, there is an exercise that when completed will allow the saxophonist to know if the throat is open when playing.

Open Throat Exercise

To simulate the feeling of playing with an open throat, saxophonists should practice speaking in the lowest voice possible. Speaking in a low voice places the throat in the optimum open position, allowing air to flow freely from the lungs. Saxophonists should remember the feeling of the throat position when speaking in a low voice and reproduce that feeling when performing. If this exercise is performed every time the saxophonist practices, in a short time playing with an open throat will become a natural part of the performer's routine.

SECRET 25: DEVELOPING THROAT FLEXIBILITY

An open, flexible throat is a great asset since it gives saxophonists the ability to adjust the intonation of a pitch without moving the embouchure, to play smoothly between registers, and also to bend notes, which is often required in certain performance styles. A flexible throat can be developed through the correct, consistent practice of appropriate exercises and patience.

Throat Flexibility Exercises

An exercise that will develop throat flexibility is to take only the mouthpiece and play a Concert C♯. Next, practice bending this note down chromatically one half step to a Concert C and then back up to the Concert C♯ using only the throat muscles. Saxophonists should make sure not to bend notes by lowering and raising the jaw. Now start on the Concert C♯ and bend it down a whole step to a Concert B then back up to the Concert C♯. Continue bending the Concert C♯ down, increasing the interval one half step each time, and then back up until the largest interval possible can be produced. This exercise can also be practiced on the saxophone with a starting note of high forked F following the same procedure described when using the mouthpiece alone. Remember to slur both exercises bending the notes with only the throat muscles.

Throat Flexibility Exercise 1
Play Using Only the Mouthpiece

Throat Flexibility Exercise 2
Play Using Only the Forked F Fingering

SECRET 26: OVERTONE EXERCISE FOR IMPROVING TONE

Overtones are often performed as preparatory exercises for playing the altissimo register since the air direction and tongue position necessary to produce these overtones are essentially the same as those needed to produce notes in the altissimo register. However, practicing overtones can also be very beneficial in developing a more resonant tone quality. By their nature, overtones are the purest, most resonant tones as they are produced not by different fingerings, but through the use of the natural harmonic series. Because overtones are very resonant, an ideal way to improve the overall tone quality of conventional notes is to compare the two and try to increase the resonance of conventional notes to the same level as their matching overtones.

Overtone Tone Exercise 1

An exercise that will accomplish this is to first play a low B♭. Next play several overtones using the B♭ as the fundamental pitch. These tones are played using the same fingering as low B♭ and are produced by adjusting only the airstream and tongue position. The next seven overtone notes that will be produced above the low B♭ are B♭ on the middle line of the staff, F on the top line of the staff, high B♭ above the staff, palm key D, palm key F, altissimo A♭, and altissimo B♭.

Overtone Tone Exercise 1
Use Low B♭ Fingering for All Notes

Overtone Tone Exercise 2

When these notes can be produced individually using the low B♭ overtone fingering, the saxophonist should play each note twice, first using the regular fingering and then with the overtone fingering (low B♭ fingering). The note produced with the overtone fingering will be much more resonant than its counterpart played with the conventional fingering. The saxophonist should listen carefully to each note and then try to increase the resonance of the conventionally fingered note to match the resonance of the overtone note by adjusting the embouchure, tongue position, and throat position. By doing this, the resonance and tone quality of the conventionally fingered note will improve.

Overtone Tone Exercise 2
*Play These Notes as Overtones Using the Low B♭ Fingering
Play All Other Notes Using Their Regular Fingerings

In addition low B and low C can also be used as fundamental notes, which will cover almost every pitch of the middle and upper register. If saxophonists regularly practice these exercises, their tone quality will be greatly improved.

Overtone Tone Exercise 3
*Play These Notes as Overtones Using the Low B Fingering
Play All Other Notes Using Their Regular Fingerings

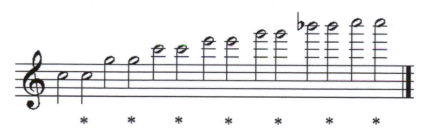

Overtone Tone Exercise 4
*Play These Notes as Overtones Using the Low C Fingering
Play All Other Notes Using Their Regular Fingerings

SECRET 27: DEVELOPING VIBRATO

Vibrato is a technique used by performers to add a more expressive, singing quality to their tone. It may be produced in several different ways, but the best method
for saxophonists to use is jaw vibrato. To produce vibrato, the jaw is lowered
and raised very similarly to the motion made when chewing while the lower lip
stays in contact with the reed. The lowering of the jaw reduces the embouchure
pressure, allowing the tone to go slightly flat. When the jaw returns to its normal
position, correct pressure is restored and the pitch is once again in tune. It is this
fluctuation in pitch, in tune and slightly flat, that produces the vibrato.

In Tune

Classical Vibrato
Vibrato Starts Immediately after Note Begins

When producing vibrato, the two basic factors manipulated by performers are
vibrato speed and width. The rate of jaw movement determines vibrato speed
while the amount of jaw movement determines vibrato width. It is important for
the saxophonist to have complete control over these two factors so vibrato can be
used to the fullest potential.

Before practicing vibrato exercises on the saxophone, the performer should first
practice the basic vibrato motion by saying the syllables *wa, wa, wa, wa*. This will
simulate the jaw movement that actually takes place when performing vibrato on
the saxophone. Once this is completed, the performer can then begin a variety of
exercises to master vibrato speed and width.

Vibrato Exercises

The first exercise for developing control over vibrato asks the performer to pick
a note and practice vibrato very slowly, making sure the jaw is correctly moving
up and down. It is important that the jaw only be allowed to move up and down to
produce the vibrato and not back and forth. A very wide vibrato width should also
be used at this time to make it easier to monitor jaw movement. This will produce
an unmusical sound but is necessary at this point in vibrato development. When
producing vibrato, saxophonists should make sure that the pitch does not go sharp
when the jaw is returned to its original position. After the saxophonist is confident
that the basic jaw movement is correct, the vibrato width can be reduced and the
speed increased.

A second exercise to practice vibrato asks the saxophonist to perform a wide variety of pulses to the beat. The performer should first practice playing vibrato with two pulses per beat, which rhythmically would be interpreted as two eighth notes. The pulses should then be increased to three, which would be triplets; four, which would be 16th notes; five; and eventually six.

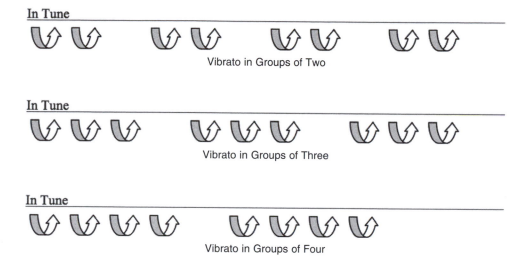

In Tune

Vibrato in Groups of Two

In Tune

Vibrato in Groups of Three

In Tune

Vibrato in Groups of Four

A third exercise for mastering vibrato is for the saxophonist to practice vibrato by starting it very slowly, gradually speeding up, and then reducing the speed. These three exercises will allow the saxophonist to develop complete control of the vibrato width and speed.

Saxophonists should also be aware that vibrato width is greatly affected by the register in which it is performed. The lower register notes will require much more jaw movement to produce the same amount of vibrato width as notes in the upper register. The saxophonist must listen and adjust the movement of the jaw to produce a consistent vibrato in all registers. Vibrato speed and width are determined by the personal preferences of the performer. By listening to accomplished artists, both instrumental and vocal, saxophonists will develop the ability to determine the appropriate vibrato speed and width for each particular piece being performed.

CHAPTER 5

Articulation Strategies

SECRET 28: CHROMATIC TONGUING EXERCISE

A quick, clean articulation is a skill needed to perform much of the advanced saxophone repertoire. Some saxophonists naturally have a fast tongue while others must work to develop this ability. The chromatic tonguing exercise is a way to develop a fast articulation and also coordinated fingers. To perform this exercise, the saxophonist must first learn the chromatic scale, making sure to use chromatic alternate fingerings discussed in Secret 31, as this will be the scale used to practice the articulation patterns. To avoid many missed notes, it is important to thoroughly learn this scale before attempting any of the articulation exercises since the mind will want to focus on the articulation patterns and not the scale. To begin the exercise, start on a third space C and play, slurring each note, chromatically down to low C then up to palm key E and return to low C. This is the basic scale range for all of the articulation patterns. Next, pick one of the 16th note articulation patterns and slowly play it using the above stated range. It is important to play each pattern slowly and cleanly in the beginning, gradually increasing the tempo over time.

Chromatic Scale in 16th Notes

16th Note Tonguing Patterns

After a saxophonist can perform all of the 16th note articulation patterns, the following triplet articulation patterns may be attempted. The format for triplet patterns is basically the same as the 16th note articulation patterns except the range of the chromatic scale is slightly different. Instead of playing up to a top note of palm key E, the saxophonist should only play up to a palm key E♭. Altering the chromatic scale range in this manner allows the saxophonist to retain the same starting and ending notes of C as when playing 16th note patterns while performing all the triplet articulation patterns.

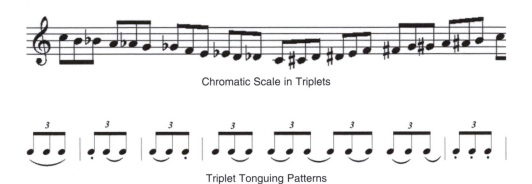

Chromatic Scale in Triplets

Triplet Tonguing Patterns

SECRET 29: DOUBLE AND TRIPLE TONGUING

The ability to double and triple tongue is very useful when articulating fast passages especially if the tempo is at a speed too fast to be single tongued. Double tonguing is a technique used to articulate notes in groups of two or four, such as eighth and 16th notes in a simple time signature. Triple tonguing is used to articulate notes in groups of three, such as triplets in a simple time signature or eighth notes in groups of three in a compound time signature. Double and triple tonguing techniques are used by many brass performers and flautists since it is relatively easy to do on these instruments. These techniques are not used as much by saxophonists since they are more difficult to master due to the saxophone's use of a mouthpiece and reed. However, with the proper technique, practice, and patience, saxophonists can learn to double and triple tongue.

Double tonguing, as the term indicates, doubles the speed a performer can single tongue by using both the tip and back of the tongue to articulate notes. When using this technique, the tongue can articulate two different syllable combinations: *da ga, da ga* or *du gu, du gu*, with the tip of the tongue touching the reed and the back of the tongue touching the roof of the mouth.

Da Ga Da Ga   Da Ga Da Ga
Double Tonguing Syllables 1

Du Gu Du Gu   Du Gu Du Gu
Double Tonguing Syllables 2

When triple tonguing, the tongue has four different syllable combinations available: *da ga da, da ga da; du gu du, du gu du; da ga da, ga da ga;* or *du gu du, gu du gu.* When performing any of these patterns, the notes should be articulated as legato as possible with the tongue not being allowed to stop the air. The tongue must also be extremely light in its movement, barely touching the reed and the roof of the mouth.

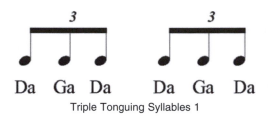
Triple Tonguing Syllables 1

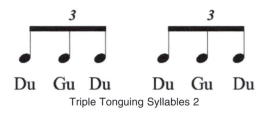
Triple Tonguing Syllables 2

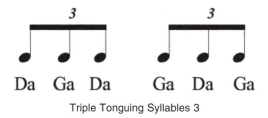
Triple Tonguing Syllables 3

Triple Tonguing Syllables 4

Exercises to develop double and triple tonguing are to play the syllabic pattern of choice first on one note, keeping the tempo slow and the articulation light. As the tongue becomes comfortable with the pattern, gradually increase the tempo, making sure to play it perfectly each time.

Next choose notes in different registers, slightly adjusting the tongue movement to produce a consistent articulation in both the upper and lower registers. The tongue will have to be considerably lighter in the upper register when performing these articulations to keep the pitch from scooping on each tongued note.

After this is accomplished, the performer should play the chromatic scale articulating the appropriate double or triple tonguing pattern four times on each note. The next step is to play the chromatic scale in 16th notes double tonguing the entire scale and playing each note only once. The chromatic scale can also be played using a triple tongue articulation pattern, tonguing the entire scale and playing each note only once. The chromatic scale range for these exercises is listed in Secret 28. After articulations are played cleanly using the chromatic scale, the performer should play a variety of scales double and triple tonguing each note. A final step would be to incorporate these new techniques into the performance of musical literature for the saxophone.

SECRET 30: THE BOUNCING TONGUE EXERCISE

When single tonguing at a slow tempo, the saxophonist has time to think about each tongue movement separately. However, when articulating at a quick tempo, the performer must abandon the idea of a separate tongue movement for each articulated note and try to group repeatedly tongued notes into larger units. By grouping the notes into larger units, the saxophonist will start the tongue thinking only of the first, initial movement; after this, the tongue will feel like it is bouncing automatically to articulate the rest of the notes in the passage. To get the tongue bouncing, the tip must be positioned very close to the reed and stay close to the reed when articulating. The tongue must also remain very relaxed, as a tongue that is tense cannot articulate quickly. This technique for articulation, when performed correctly, will dramatically increase the single tongue speed.

An exercise for developing this technique is to tongue one note, then two, three, four, five, six, seven, and finally eight. When playing this exercise, only the initial attack should be thought of. When performing the other tonguing strokes, the tongue should feel like it is lightly bouncing off the reed similar to bouncing a basketball very quickly and closely to the floor. The tongue position should be very high in the oral cavity with the tip of the tongue kept very close to the tip of the reed. When tonguing, the articulation should be very light with the minimum amount of movement. Only the tip of the tongue should move when articulating and only in upward and downward motion, not forward and backward. The tongue must also stay relaxed during this exercise since the body performs best when it is in a relaxed state.

The Bouncing Tongue Exercise

CHAPTER 6

Finger Technique Strategies

SECRET 31: CHROMATIC ALTERNATE FINGERINGS

The saxophone is designed with several alternate fingerings to be used when playing the chromatic scale or chromatic passages. These alternate fingerings, which require less finger movement, make chromatic passages easier to play. However, if a saxophonist has already learned the chromatic scale using regular fingerings, switching to the alternate fingerings may seem more difficult in the beginning. If this is the case, the performer should continue to practice the alternate fingerings since this feeling will pass quickly and soon the new fingerings will become automatic.

Three Chromatic Alternate Fingerings

There are three fingerings to be used when playing chromatically. They are side C, to be used in place of middle finger C; side B♭, to be used instead of bis key B♭; and ring F♯, to be used in place of middle finger F♯. These fingerings should be used in both registers, with or without the octave key.

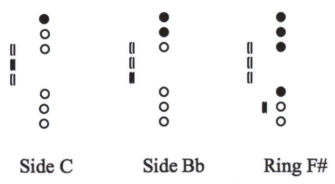

Side C   Side Bb   Ring F#

Chromatic Alternate Fingerings without Octave Key

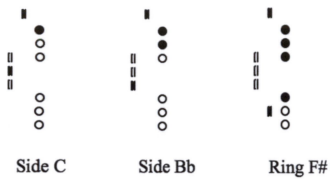

Side C   Side Bb   Ring F#

Chromatic Alternate Fingerings with Octave Key

SECRET 32: ALTERNATE B♭ FINGERINGS

When playing the note B♭, located on the third line of the staff or the octave above, there are four fingerings available for the saxophonist to choose from: side B♭, bis key B♭, 1&1 B♭ (the first finger in each hand is depressed), and 1&2 B♭ (the left-hand first finger and the right-hand middle finger are depressed). It is important for performers to know which fingering to use based on how the B♭ is approached and resolved.

Alternate B♭ Guidelines

There are several general guidelines for deciding which B♭ fingering to use. The first guideline is when approaching and resolving B♭ chromatically (A to B♭ to B), the side B♭ fingering should be used. The second guideline is when leaping to B♭ and resolving by leap or chromatically, the bis key B♭ fingering should be used. The third guideline is the 1&1 B♭ or 1&2 B♭ fingerings are rarely used with the exception of certain patterns like B to B♭ to B, moving down one half step and then back up. These rules are basically suggestions to assist the saxophonist in developing technique. Many saxophonists use these suggestions when performing, but others have developed their own system for fingering B♭. The most important thing is that saxophonists have the technique to play quickly and cleanly. How this is achieved is a personal choice.

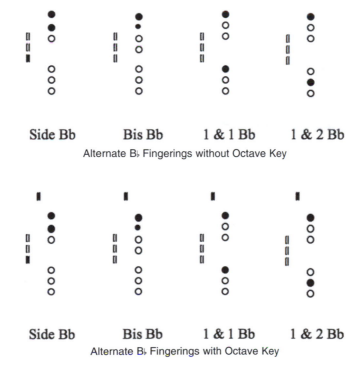

Side Bb   Bis Bb   1 & 1 Bb   1 & 2 Bb

Alternate B♭ Fingerings without Octave Key

Side Bb   Bis Bb   1 & 1 Bb   1 & 2 Bb

Alternate B♭ Fingerings with Octave Key

SECRET 33: HOLDING DOWN THE PINKY FINGERS

The saxophone is designed with a mechanism that allows performers to hold down their pinky fingers (left-hand G♯ or low C♯ and right-hand D♯) even when playing notes other than G♯ and D♯. The saxophone is unique in this aspect since holding down both pinky fingers on other woodwind instruments renders them unplayable. This design is of great assistance when playing in key signatures that contain G♯ and D♯ since one or both of the pinky fingers can be held down for entire musical passages. Implementing this technique allows the saxophonist to never miss a G♯ or D♯ because the pinky fingers are already in place before these notes are played. Another big advantage is the coordination required to finger G♯ and D♯ is improved, allowing the performer to play these notes more quickly and cleanly with less practice.

Developing Pinky Technique

To develop this technique, the saxophonist should start first by practicing the major scales E, B, F♯, and C♯ while holding the pinky fingers down for the entire scale. The A scale can also be practiced but with only the right-hand pinky finger held down. After these scales have been mastered, the performer can then begin practicing technical exercises, études, and finally the saxophone repertoire utilizing this technique. It should be noted that when this technique is first attempted, saxophonists might feel uncomfortable holding down their pinky fingers while playing notes other than G♯ and D♯. However, if this technique is consistently practiced, it will become second nature, greatly improving speed and accuracy.

Pinky Technique 1
Hold Down Left- (G♯) and Right-Hand (D♯) Pinky Fingers for the Entire Scale

Pinky Technique 2
Hold Down Left- (C♯) and Right-Hand (D♯) Pinky Fingers for the Entire Scale

After playing the low C♯, continue to hold the left-hand pinky finger down on the low C♯ fingering as this will also sharp all the Gs in the scale. Also hold down the right-hand pinky finger as this will sharp all the Ds in the scale.

SECRET 34: FORKED E AND F

The saxophone is designed with palm keys for use in playing the upper register notes D, D♯, E, and F. The palm keys work well when approaching these notes either chromatically or by step. However, when leaping to these notes, the palm keys can be somewhat awkward to use. To improve this situation, the saxophone also has in its design another way to finger high E and F. These alternate fingerings, called forked E and forked F, use the key located directly above the left-hand index B fingering and make it much easier to leap to these notes, especially from the note high C.

In addition to making leaps easier, the forked fingerings also assist the saxophonist when playing musical passages that ascend into the altissimo register. In many cases, the forked fingerings are technically easier to perform than the palm keys when playing into the altissimo register and the high tongue position required to produce forked E and F notes is very similar to the tongue position needed to produce notes in the altissimo register. By playing forked E and F fingerings, the tongue is already in position for playing in the altissimo register.

Forked E and F Fingerings

To play a forked E, the left-hand index finger depresses the key directly above the B fingering key along with the octave key and the left-hand middle and ring finger keys. Forked F uses the exact same fingering as forked E except the left-hand ring finger is not depressed. Forked E and F fingerings are used primarily when leaping from the note C and require much less finger movement.

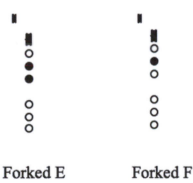

Forked E   Forked F

Forked E and F Fingerings

Instead of using all the palm keys to play a high F when leaping from high C, the forked F fingering requires only that the left-hand index finger be added to the existing high C fingering, making this leap much easier to play. The same is true for leaping to high E from high C. In this case, adding the left-hand index finger and the left-hand ring finger to the existing high C fingering is all that is needed to perform the leap. However, when first performing forked fingerings, the forked E and F may not respond as well as the palm key fingerings for these notes. This response problem can be corrected by making sure the back of the tongue is in a high position, similar to saying the words *he* or *her*. Taking a little more mouthpiece into the mouth may also assist in solving this problem. It should be noted that forked E and F fingerings have a slight difference in tone quality than their palm key equivalents and their intonation tendencies may also be different. However, these limitations are greatly outweighed by the benefits of using forked fingerings, prompting many saxophonists to frequently use them.

SECRET 35: DEVELOPING FINGER SPEED

Quick finger speed is a skill that is necessary to perform much of the advanced saxophone literature and is sometimes a problem for advancing saxophonists. However, finger speed is not difficult to develop as long as the performer has the proper hand position and finger height and a correct practice routine.

The first step in developing finger speed is to have the proper hand position. The left-hand position should be relaxed with the thumb resting comfortably on the thumb pad below the octave key. It is important that when depressing the octave key, the thumb does so by rolling into position and never losing contact with the thumb pad. Some saxophonists incorrectly lift the thumb off the thumb pad when depressing the octave key, which causes technique problems when changing registers. The left-hand fingers should be curved with their tips placed on the appropriate keys. The left-hand pinky finger should rest lightly on the G♯ key.

The right hand should be relaxed and form the shape of a C with the thumb tucked underneath the thumb rest. Saxophonists should be careful not to allow too much of the thumb to slide under the thumb rest as this will put the right-hand fingers in an incorrect position. The tips of the right-hand fingers should be placed on the appropriate keys with the right-hand pinky finger resting lightly on the D♯ key. Placing the hands in the correct position is the first step to developing finger speed.

Another very important factor in developing finger speed is finger height. Many saxophonists lift their fingers completely off the keys when performing. This not only slows down finger speed but also causes problems with coordination, as each lifted finger must move a different distance to reach the key. However, when playing notes that require the palm keys to be depressed, it will be necessary to lift the fingers slightly from the keys. When doing this, the saxophonist should strive to keep the fingers as close to their original position as possible so movement is kept to a minimum.

A third factor in developing finger speed is following a correct practice routine. When practicing for speed, the fingers must be relaxed and remain on the keys. Scales and melodic patterns must be practiced slowly and played perfectly every time. If the saxophonist is making mistakes or lifting the fingers from the keys, the tempo should be slowed down further until a speed is found where the scale or pattern can be played perfectly. A mirror should also be used and positioned in a manner that the performer can see the fingers while playing. This will be of great assistance in determining if all the fingers are staying in the correct position. In addition, a metronome must be used to ensure that notes are being played evenly and at a steady tempo.

When working for speed, scales and patterns should be broken down into smaller units at first and played perfectly many times using a metronome. This technique will develop what is known as muscle memory, which means that the fingers will move to the appropriate keys at the appropriate time with little or no thought. As a saxophonist masters a scale or melodic pattern and can play it at least three consecutive times without making a mistake, the tempo can be slightly increased at a rate of two or three metronome markings before beginning the pattern again. By doing this, the saxophonist ensures that as the pattern becomes faster, it is still being played correctly. By playing passages slowly, evenly, and perfectly while keeping the fingers on the keys and gradually increasing the tempo, saxophonists will greatly improve their finger speed.

Finger Speed Pattern 1

Finger Speed Pattern 2

Finger Speed Pattern 3

SECRET 36: USING THE METRONOME

The metronome is one of the most important tools for developing technique on the saxophone. Most saxophonists who practice without a metronome are shocked when they discover how poor their sense of time is. However, they are also happily surprised when they discover how quickly improvement takes place once practicing with a metronome begins.

A metronome can be used in several ways to improve a saxophonist's sense of time and technique. The first and most common use of a metronome is to have it click on the beat, allowing the performer to develop a steady tempo by feeling each beat of a measure. This strategy works well for playing notes of longer durations such as whole, half, quarter, and eighth notes.

However, when playing passages that contain 16th notes, another technique may be more beneficial. If the metronome clicks only on the beat when playing groups of four 16th notes, only the first note of each group has to line up with the click. This may allow the other three 16th notes to be somewhat uneven, especially if being performed at a slower tempo. A better way of using the metronome in this case is to double its speed, having it click on the beats and the upbeats of each measure. By doing this, every other 16th note has to line up with a metronome click, ensuring that all notes are played evenly and at a steady tempo.

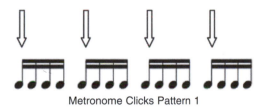
Metronome Clicks Pattern 1

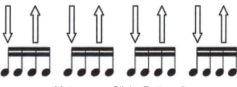
Metronome Clicks Pattern 2

CHAPTER 7

Altissimo Strategies

SECRET 37: OVERTONE EXERCISE FOR DEVELOPING THE ALTISSIMO REGISTER

The ability to play notes in the altissimo register is a highly desirable skill for most saxophonists. However, when undertaking this endeavor, many saxophonists simply look up the fingerings for altissimo notes in a fingering chart and attempt to play them with no idea of what changes are necessary in the tongue position and airstream. When this strategy does not work, some saxophonists give up, never realizing that there are exercises, when properly practiced, that will develop the skills necessary to play in the altissimo register.

One exercise that will develop the altissimo register requires the playing of overtones. Overtones are harmonic notes that are played over a low fundamental note by adjusting the tongue position and airstream instead of using different fingerings. Learning to play different pitches by only changing the tongue position and airstream is precisely the skill needed to play in the altissimo register. To begin the altissimo overtone exercise, the saxophonist first plays a low B♭ below the staff. Then the B♭ an octave above located on the third line of the staff is played using the same fingering as low B♭. The new note is played only by adjusting the back of the tongue to a higher position in the oral cavity. This tongue adjustment will feel like saying the word *he* or *her*. Each note should also be started with a breath attack and not tongued since this will cause additional movement of the tongue. Next, the F on the fifth line of the staff is played only by moving the tongue to a higher position. This process continues, playing the entire overtone series by adjusting the tongue to a higher position but using the low B♭ fingering.

This exercise can also be performed with low B and low C as fundamental notes. By developing the ability to play overtones, the saxophonist will now have the skills necessary to play in the altissimo register.

Overtone Exercise 1
Use Low B♭ Fingering for All Notes

Overtone Exercise 2
Use Low B Fingering for All Notes

Overtone Exercise 3
Use Low C Fingering for All Notes

SECRET 38: ALTISSIMO TECHNIQUE FINGERINGS

When playing in the altissimo register, the most important factors are tongue position, airstream, and the ability to hear the pitch before it is played. After these issues are resolved, the proper altissimo fingerings should be examined. For each altissimo note, there are several possible fingering choices. Some fingerings may produce a better tone while others are easier to play technically. Initially, saxophonists should try various fingering combinations to see which ones they prefer the most. Eventually they will develop a set of fingering combinations that work best for them in almost every performance situation.

Since altissimo fingerings are somewhat more difficult to perform when compared to other note fingerings, saxophonists are sometimes limited in their ability to play quickly in this register. The following set of altissimo fingerings are designed for speed and will give the saxophonist the agility that is sometimes lacking when playing chromatically in the altissimo register.

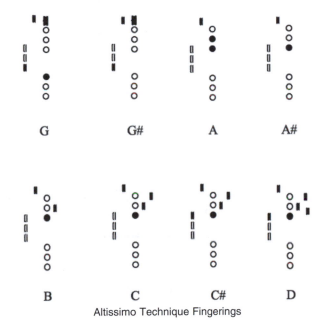

Altissimo Technique Fingerings

SECRET 39: ALTISSIMO FINGER EXERCISES

Once the tongue position, airstream, and note fingerings have been established, saxophonists should practice to develop speed and agility in the altissimo register. There are many ways to develop this technique, but several of the most common exercises are detailed below.

One exercise to develop fluency in the altissimo register is to play all the major scales and arpeggios into this range. This means that a C major scale and arpeggio that is normally played two octaves should now be played three octaves. The saxophonist should use forked E and F fingerings when playing scales into the altissimo register when appropriate as these fingerings prepare the performer's tongue position and airstream for this register. The chromatic scale can also be practiced with this extended range.

C Major Scale Three Octaves

C Major Arpeggio Three Octaves

Chromatic Scale Three Octaves

Another exercise is to play the same note in all available octaves. An example would be to play low C, then C on the third space of the staff, then high C above the staff, and finally altissimo C.

Playing C in All Registers

Other exercises are to play simple folk or children's tunes first in a lower octave and then in the altissimo register. This can be done by writing the tunes out or by playing them by ear.

"Mary Had a Little Lamb." *Public Domain*

"Mary Had a Little Lamb" Altissimo Register. *Public Domain*

CHAPTER 8

Extended Technique Strategies

SECRET 40: CIRCULAR BREATHING

Circular breathing is an extended technique used by performers when there is no place in a musical passage to take a breath. This technique allows the saxophonist to take a breath while continuing to sustain the notes currently being played. When utilizing circular breathing, the performer pushes air into the instrument with the cheek muscles while at the same time breathing in through the nose. This technique keeps a constant airflow moving into the instrument while allowing the saxophonist an opportunity to take breaths when needed.

Circular breathing is a technique rarely needed in the performance of saxophone literature since most of the repertoire has places to breathe especially at the ends of phrases. However, there are certain pieces, such as Eugene Bozza's *Improvisation et Caprice* and others, where this technique is very useful.

Circular breathing is also used by performers in commercial and jazz music as a way of showing their mastery of the instrument. This technique, which is somewhat of a novelty, can be a useful tool when used properly in performance.

Learning to Circular Breathe

To develop the ability to circular breathe, the saxophonist should practice the following procedures.

1. Inhale through the nose and then blow air out of the mouth while allowing the cheeks to fill with air and puff out.
2. Inhale through the nose, while keeping the mouth closed. Next, blow air into the oral cavity, allowing the cheeks to fill with air and puff out. Keep the mouth closed so no air can escape. Now slowly force the air contained in

the cheeks out of the mouth by squeezing the cheeks back into their original position.

3. Repeat step 2 but when forcing the air out of the mouth with the cheeks, also inhale through the nose.

4. Using a glass filled with water and a drinking straw, inhale through the nose and begin blowing bubbles into the glass of water through the drinking straw. Allow the cheeks to fill with air and puff out while doing this. Next, force air into the straw by squeezing the cheeks back to their original position. At the same, inhale quickly through the nose. When the air is gone from the cheeks, begin blowing air into the straw from the lungs. The air bubbles should not stop at any time during this process.

5. Using only the mouthpiece and neck of the saxophone, inhale through the nose and begin a tone by blowing into the mouthpiece. Allow the cheeks to fill with air and puff out while doing this. Next, force air into the mouthpiece by squeezing the cheeks back to their original position. At the same time, inhale quickly through the nose. When the air is gone from the cheeks, begin blowing air into the mouthpiece from the lungs. The tone being produced should not stop at any time during this process. Using a softer reed when practicing this exercise will make it easier.

6. Assemble the saxophone and repeat step 5 while fingering an open C♯ on the third space of the staff. When successfully circular breathing on this note, continue to practice on the notes C, B, B♭, A, A♭, and G, working down chromatically from C♯.

7. Practice circular breathing while trilling between any of the notes listed in step 6.

8. Practice circular breathing by playing the top tetrachord of a C major scale. Starting on the note G, play the notes G, A, B, C, ascending and then descending back down to the G. Continuously repeat this pattern using circular breathing when needed.

9. Practice circular breathing while playing a G major scale. Starting on G, continuously play the G major scale up to the ninth, which is the note A, and then back down using circular breathing when needed.

10. Practice circular breathing while playing a variety of scales and scale patterns.

By practicing these procedures, the saxophonist will develop the ability to circular breathe and over time become comfortable enough with this technique to begin using it in performances.

SECRET 41: SLAP TONGUING

Slap tonguing is an extended technique used by saxophonists that produces a unique popping sound when articulating notes in a pizzicato style. This effect, sometimes called for in contemporary saxophone literature, is notated either by an X note head or by placing a + sign below the note along with the words *slap tongue*. Commercial and jazz performers also use this technique to show mastery of their instrument and to create more interesting solos.

Slap Tonguing

Learning to Slap Tongue

Before trying to slap tongue on the saxophone, the performer should first practice this technique by simulating the tongue movement against the roof of the mouth. To do this, the tongue should be pressed flat against the roof of the mouth just behind the front teeth.

Next, the tongue should be quickly and forcefully pulled downward, producing a popping sound. No air is blown from the lungs while completing this movement as the popping sound is made from the release of suction created between the tongue and the roof of the mouth. Continue practicing this exercise, striving to make the popping sound as loud as possible.

To produce a slap tongue on the saxophone, the performer first fingers the note to be tongued, then places the tongue flat against the reed, covering the surface approximately one half inch in from the tip. A lower register note is suggested since slap tonguing is easier to produce on these notes. Next the middle of the tongue is pulled away from the reed while keeping the tongue's sides and tip in place. This creates an area of suction between the reed and tongue that when released by forcefully pulling the tongue downward creates a popping or slapping sound. When slap tonguing, no air actually enters the mouthpiece. However, depending upon how much resonance is desired, a slight puff of air may be added to the tongue movement.

SECRET 42: FLUTTER TONGUING

Flutter tonguing is an extended technique used by saxophonists to change the timbre of a note. Unlike other types of articulation, flutter tonguing is not actually used to articulate notes in the traditional sense but is used to modify the tone, giving it a raspy, growling timbre. This technique, used both in classical, commercial, and jazz styles, is a very effective way of creating musical expression and interest. The standard notation for flutter tonguing is to write the note with three beams through the stem with f. t. or its equivalent in a foreign language written above to avoid confusion.

Flutter Tonguing

Learning to Flutter Tongue

There are two methods of flutter tonguing available to the performer. In the first method, flutter tonguing is produced by fluttering the tip of the tongue against the roof of the mouth just behind the front teeth using a rolled R movement. For some saxophonists, this method of flutter tonguing is not possible because they cannot roll the tongue in an R fashion. A second method of flutter tonguing is to vibrate the back of the tongue against the roof of the mouth in a movement similar to gargling. This technique produces a weaker flutter tongue but allows those performers who cannot roll their Rs a way to produce the effect.

To develop the ability to flutter tongue, a performer should first try to produce a rolled R sound by fluttering the tip of the tongue against the roof of the mouth without using the instrument. If this cannot be done after some practice, the second method of vibrating the back of the tongue against the roof of the mouth similar to gargling should be tried. After being successful at one of these methods, an attempt to flutter tongue should be attempted using just the saxophone mouthpiece and neck. If using the first method, start the tone and then begin rolling the tongue in an R movement against the roof of the mouth while blowing a narrow stream of fast-moving air into the mouthpiece. The back of the tongue will feel very high in the oral cavity as if saying the word *her*. Make sure not to touch the reed with the tongue, as this will stop the tone.

If using method two, start the tone and then begin vibrating the back of the tongue against the roof of the mouth while blowing a strong, narrow stream of air into the mouthpiece, again not allowing the tongue to touch the reed. After being successful at one of these methods, the saxophone can be assembled and the performer can begin practicing flutter tonguing with the instrument. Notes in the mid and low range should be practiced first since the tones are easier to flutter tongue than notes in the upper register. Once the performer feels comfortable with these notes, flutter tonguing can be expanded into the upper register, making sure to lighten the tongue movement as the notes ascend.

SECRET 43: MULTIPHONICS

Multiphonics is an extended saxophone technique used in classical, commercial, and jazz styles. The term *multiphonics*, which means multiple tones, is used to play several harmonic notes at once on what is normally considered a monophonic, or single note, instrument. Multiphonics are produced by using alternate fingerings, adjusting the embouchure, and changing the voicing of the throat. The sound of a multiphonic note is somewhat shocking when first heard since the tone has an aggressive harshness to it that sounds completely different from a traditional note. This is perhaps the reason why multiphonics is a popular technique used in many styles of contemporary music.

Multiphonic Fingerings

There are many multiphonic fingerings, some of which are more difficult to produce than others. Listed below are several common multiphonic fingerings that are easy to finger and sound. The fundamental pitch for each multiphonic is placed below each fingering. This should help the saxophonist when attempting to sound the multiphonic since this pitch will sound the loudest when the multiphonic is correctly produced. These fingerings will give the advancing saxophonist a good introduction to playing multiphonics on his or her instrument.

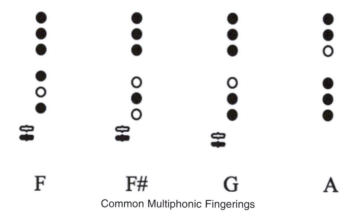

Common Multiphonic Fingerings

CHAPTER 9

Jazz Techniques

SECRET 44: THE STRAIGHT LIP EMBOUCHURE

When performing in the classical style, most saxophonists strive for a dark, warm symphonic tone, which allows the saxophone to blend well with other orchestral and band instruments. This is accomplished by first developing a proper tonal concept and then through the use of a classical saxophone mouthpiece and traditional embouchure. In a traditional classical embouchure, the lower lip covers a portion of the lower teeth in varying amounts depending upon the tonal concept of the saxophonist. The more lip that is allowed to cover the teeth and come into contact with the reed, the darker, more muted the tone. When playing in the classical style, this tone may be desirable, but when performing in the jazz style, this sound may be exactly opposite of what is desired. To correct this situation, when classical saxophonists play in the jazz style, many times they switch to a jazz mouthpiece and use a softer reed to brighten the tone. For those saxophonists who desire an even brighter and more authentic jazz tone, a straight lip embouchure may also be used.

Commercial and jazz saxophonists most commonly use the straight lip embouchure because it produces a tone that is highly desired in these styles of music. When forming a straight lip embouchure, the lower lip is not allowed to fold over and cover any portion of the lower teeth as in the classical embouchure. The lower lip maintains a position in front of the lower teeth, reducing the amount of surface contact with the reed and brightening the sound. To form a straight lip embouchure, the lips form an O similar to the shape made when whistling. When the mouthpiece is inserted in the mouth, it is not allowed to pull any of the lower lip in with it. As a result, the lip has less surface contact with the reed and there is less embouchure pressure, especially from the lower teeth and jaw. By playing with less pressure, the reed is allowed to vibrate more freely, creating a brighter, more resonant tone.

The straight lip embouchure, and the amount of embouchure pressure produced when using it, is perhaps the major difference between the embouchures of classical and jazz saxophonists. Classical performers tend to play with slightly more embouchure pressure from the lower lip, lower teeth, and jaw than jazz performers due to the use of a traditional embouchure. To compare these two types of embouchures, the saxophonist should play a long tone using only the mouthpiece and neck and using a traditional embouchure, making sure to place the mouthpiece on the neck at the spot where the instrument is normally in tune. When using a traditional embouchure, the long tone pitch produced should be a Concert A♭. Next, the saxophonist should play a long tone using the straight lip embouchure, which uses less embouchure pressure. The pitch produced will be lower, around a Concert G.

Saxophonists who are involved in playing both classical and jazz styles may find the use of both types of embouchures very beneficial. However, it can be difficult to switch back and forth between the two since they are quite different. In addition, if a saxophonist decides to switch between the two, an attempt should not be tried until one of the embouchures has clearly been established as the primary setup. This suggestion is recommended to avoid confusion between the two embouchures. By developing both the traditional and straight lip embouchures, saxophonists will be much more adept in playing in both classical and jazz styles.

SECRET 45: SUB-TONING

When performing in the classical style, saxophonists strive to maintain a consistent timbre for each note throughout the entire range of the saxophone. This concept is most evident when listening to classical saxophonists play in the lower range of the instrument. These lower register notes, which have the same timbre as notes in the middle and upper range of the saxophone, are not manipulated in any way to reduce the amount of edge in the tone.

Sub-toning is a technique used by saxophonists to manipulate the timbre of notes in the lower register by removing all the edge from the sound. This technique, which is sometimes called for in classical saxophone literature, is most commonly used in the performance of jazz. When performing in the jazz style, sub-toning is used when performing standard jazz literature and especially in jazz ballads.

To sub-tone in the lower register, the saxophonist pulls the lower jaw back toward the face while dropping it slightly downward. These movements reduce the amount of embouchure pressure on the mouthpiece while increasing the amount of lower lip on the reed, giving the note a sub-tone quality. This technique, while used by many jazz performers, is outside the classic saxophone style and should not be used when performing the classical repertoire unless specified.

Also, since this is an advanced technique, beginning saxophonists should avoid using it when first learning to form the embouchure, as it could lead to stability problems. Only after the embouchure has been thoroughly established should performers begin to attempt this technique. In addition, saxophonists should always be consciously aware when using this technique so it does not become a habit used indiscriminately every time the lower register is played. If sub-toning becomes a habit, it can be very difficult to break later on when the saxophonist is performing in the classical style and does not wish to use it. However, developing this technique is a must for saxophonists who aspire to play in the jazz style. When sub-toning is performed correctly and used within the appropriate context, it provides the saxophonist with a new expressive technique for the lower register.

SECRET 46: SWINGING

Some saxophonists easily grasp the concept of swinging while others seem to struggle. In reality, swinging is not a difficult concept to understand if explained correctly. However, applying this concept to performance may be more difficult. When reading pairs of eighth notes in classical music, the beat is divided equally between the two. When reading music in a swing style, the saxophonist will see pairs of eighth notes written in the same manner as in classical music. However, somewhere on the written page will be directions for the performer to swing these notes. This requires the saxophonist to interpret the notation by actually playing rhythms that are not written on the page. When playing a pair of eighth notes in a swing style, the saxophonist is actually performing the rhythm of three triplet eighth notes with the first two tied together. The tying of the first two triplet eighth notes allows the rhythm to swing by dividing the beat into two unequal divisions. The first eighth note is worth two-thirds of the beat while the last eighth note is worth one-third of the beat.

Tied Eighth/Eighth Triplet = Quarter/Eighth Triplet = Swing Eighth Notes

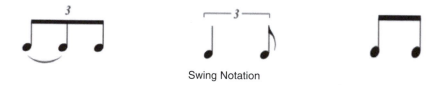

Swing Notation

Learning to Swing

When initially practicing swing eighth notes, the saxophonist should first count and then slowly play three triplet eighth notes to establish an even triplet feel.

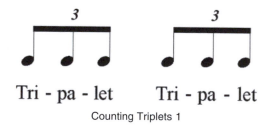

Tri - pa - let   Tri - pa - let

Counting Triplets 1

When this rhythm feels comfortable, then count and play the actual swing eighth note pattern of tri-plet, tri-plet with the "tri" getting two-thirds of the beat while the "plet" gets one-third.

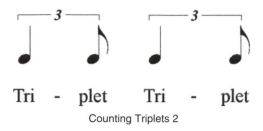

Tri - plet   Tri - plet

Counting Triplets 2

Once this basic swing feel has been developed, the saxophonist should practice performing a variety of scales, patterns, exercises, and études in the swing style at a variety of tempi.

Swinging at Different Tempi

Perhaps the most difficult aspect of swinging and the problem that troubles many performers is the ability to swing at a variety of tempi. When performing at a slow tempo, saxophonists will play eighth notes using the triplet division discussed earlier. However, as the tempo becomes faster, the eighth notes must be played more evenly to retain a legato, flowing jazz style. At very fast tempi, swing eighth notes do not actually swing at all but are divided and played evenly. This concept of playing the eighth notes more evenly as the tempo increases causes problems for multitudes of performers. Many times saxophonists will try to retain the triplet division used at a slow tempo for faster tunes, producing an awkward, unnatural, overly swung style. Other times performers will play eighth notes too evenly at a slow tempo, causing the tune not to swing enough.

The ability to know how much to swing eighth notes at a variety of tempi and to get the musical line to swing hard and sound natural is one of the most difficult tasks jazz saxophonists have to perform. To develop this ability, saxophonists should first listen to recordings of master jazz musicians improvising at a variety of tempi, paying close attention to how the eighth notes are played and what changes are made from one tempo to another. To assist in this process, the performer should either transcribe or attain a transcription of the solos being listened to. Next saxophonists should imitate these musicians, trying to perform the musical lines in exactly the same manner including dynamics and articulations. Finally the performer should play along with the recordings to get a feel for how the lines are phrased. If possible, saxophonists should record themselves performing these solos and compare their performance to the original. By practicing this way, the ability to swing at a variety of tempi will be developed and become a natural part of a saxophonist's playing style.

SECRET 47: BACK-ACCENT TONGUING

When performing in a swing jazz style, using the correct articulation is very important. Performing with the proper articulation will assist the musical lines with clarity, improve their swing feel, and provide intensity and interest. When comparing performances of professional jazz performers to that of advancing saxophonists, articulation is one aspect that dramatically separates the two.

In many jazz arrangements, specific articulations are not notated in the ensemble parts, and when playing an improvised solo, performers must create their own articulations based upon their knowledge of articulation style, the tempo of the tune, and the rhythms they choose to play. As a result, many saxophonists tongue every note when performing tunes at slower tempi, slur every note on faster tunes, or randomly tongue and slur notes in their improvised solos. Articulating in this manner inhibits the musical performance and is also a misrepresentation of jazz performance traditions. Therefore, it should be avoided.

When playing jazz, the method of articulation that should be used is called back-accent tonguing. This style of tonguing is the most commonly used articulation when playing swing music. Back-accent tonguing is very easy to understand and will quickly improve the saxophonist's ability to perform clean lines and authentic-sounding musical phrases. When using this articulation, the saxophonist lightly tongues each note on the upbeat and slurs to the note on the beat. For example in a series of eighth notes starting on the upbeat, the saxophonist should tongue the first eighth note in the series and then slur to the note on the beat. This pattern should be repeated until the series of eighth notes ends.

Back-Accent Tonguing 1

If a series of eighth notes begins on the beat, the saxophonist should tongue the first two eighth notes in the series—the first eighth note on the beat to start the series and also the second eighth note since it is on the upbeat—and then slur to the next note on the beat.

Back-Accent Tonguing 2

Back-accent tonguing assists the musical phrase in swinging because all upbeat notes are being lightly tongued while all notes on the beats are being slurred. It should be emphasized that when using this style of articulation, the saxophonist should lightly tongue each upbeat eighth note and play in a legato style. Notes should be sustained at all times, producing a continuous flow of sound. When saxophonists incorrectly perform back-accent tonguing, the two most common problems are tonguing too hard and allowing the tone to stop between the slurred note on the beat and the tongued note on the following upbeat.

Since the concept of back-accent tonguing is easy to understand and produces authentically articulated phrases, it is also a great tool to use when performing in the saxophone section of a jazz ensemble. If each member of the section understands and correctly uses back-accent tonguing, the saxophone section will have a consistent articulation that promotes hard swinging lines with a minimum amount of practice.

To practice back-accent tonguing, saxophonists should first practice a variety of scales and modes used for jazz improvisation to get accustomed to using this style of articulation. Then this articulation can be incorporated into playing ensemble parts and improvisation. After back-accent tonguing has been mastered, saxophonists may want to vary their articulation, customizing it based upon the notes and specific rhythms being played and also through imitation of articulations performed by prominent jazz players.

SECRET 48: HALF TONGUING

Half tonguing is a style of articulation used in the performance of jazz that adds much expression to a musical phrase and also promotes a swing feel. It is used by many jazz masters as well as prominent professional saxophonists and will greatly enhance a performer's playing style. Half tonguing is basically a tool for muting specific notes in a jazz phrase using the tongue instead of manipulating the airstream. Muting specific notes at key points in a musical phrase allows the phrase to swing harder and also brings more attention to the melodic notes enhancing the melodic line. Also, this method of muting notes is much more efficient than using the airstream since when performing fast, articulated lines, it is very difficult to manipulate single notes by adjusting the airflow.

To produce a half-tongued note, saxophonists should lightly touch and hold the tongue against the reed for the entire duration of a note without allowing the note to stop sounding. In other words, the tongue is lightly held against the reed, but the reed is not allowed to stop vibrating. This may be difficult to accomplish at first since the reed will stop vibrating if too much of the tongue touches it or if the tongue is pressed too firmly against it. In addition, there is not a standard method for half tonguing since saxophonists usually develop their own technique, determining for themselves what part and how much of the tongue touches the reed. However, one successful method of accomplishing this articulation uses the side of the tongue to touch the side of the reed. By holding the side of the tongue against the side of the reed, there is less surface area contact, promoting reed vibration. Also, when half tonguing, using a forceful, narrow stream of air will make this articulation easier.

To develop the ability to half tongue, saxophonists should first think and say the syllables *doo-n, doo-n*. This will simulate the tongue movement that occurs when actually performing the half-tongued articulation. Next, the performer should attempt to half tongue a note in the middle register of the instrument by initially playing and holding the selected note. After the note is started with a normal tongued articulation, the saxophonist can slowly move one side of the tongue toward one side of the reed, allowing it to lightly touch. It does not matter which side of the tongue or which side of the reed is used as long as the side tip of the tongue is used to touch the reed. If the left side tip of the tongue is preferred, it should touch the right side of the reed, or if the right side tip of the tongue is used, it should touch the left side of the reed. When lightly touching and then holding the tongue to the reed, the saxophonist should pay close attention to the reed's vibration, making sure it does not stop. If the reed stops vibrating, the tongue should be pulled away and the process started over.

After half tonguing has been mastered on notes in the middle register, the saxophonist can expand this articulation to notes in the upper and lower registers. The next step is to half tongue notes of shorter duration and to develop coordination between the tongue and the fingers. One exercise for doing this is to slowly play a G major scale in eighth notes, tonguing the notes on the beats and half tonguing the notes on the upbeats. After this pattern becomes natural, it can be performed using other major scales.

A jazz articulation pattern that is commonly used in running eighth note lines combines half tonguing with back-accent tonguing to produce a clean, hard swinging phrase. In this pattern, back-accent tonguing is used to start a series of eighth notes but on the fourth note of the series, the note is half tongued instead of being slurred. When performing this articulation pattern the saxophonist should think of the syllables *doo-doo-oo-n*.

Half Tonguing Pattern 1

Practice this pattern using the following scale pattern.

Half Tonguing Pattern 1 C Major Scale

Another common jazz articulation combines half tonguing with back-accent tonguing using the same basic pattern previously discussed but in this articulation, the second note in the series is half tongued instead of the fourth. Syllables for this pattern are *doo-n-oo-doo*.

Half Tonguing Pattern 2

Practice this articulation using the following arpeggio pattern.

Half Tonguing Pattern 2 C Arpeggio

The process of half tonguing may feel strange and even uncomfortable at first due to holding the tongue against a vibrating reed. However, after a short period of time, the tongue will become accustomed to the vibrating reed and these sensations will go away.

SECRET 49: GHOSTED NOTES

Ghosting notes is a technique used in almost all genres of music including jazz and commercial styles. This technique is used to deaden specific notes in a musical phrase, allowing it to swing harder, and also adds much interest and character. Ghosted notes have the same rhythmic value as notes that are not ghosted but are performed with little or no sound. When playing a ghosted note, the saxophonist fingers the note, giving it the appropriate rhythmic duration, but does not allow the note to sound as loudly as other surrounding notes. Some performers refer to this technique as swallowing the note. The exact volume of a ghosted note varies depending upon the performer's style and the musical situation involved. Some ghosted notes may be inaudible while others are heard only slightly. In musical notation, a ghosted note is usually written with an X in place of the normal note head or by placing the note head in parentheses.

There are several ways to produce ghosted notes on the saxophone. One method, which produces an inaudible, implied note, is accomplished by greatly reducing the airflow into the instrument while fingering the ghosted note. When using this technique, the saxophonist simply blows much less air or no air into the instrument to produce the ghosted note. This method works well when playing ghosted eighth notes at slower tempi since it allows the performer time to adjust the airflow for a specific note.

Another method that produces an inaudible note is one where the tongue is used to stop the reed while the ghosted note is being fingered. This approach works better than the first when playing eighth notes at faster speeds since it is much easier to stop the reed with the tongue than to adjust the airflow.

A third method of ghosting notes is to finger the note while using half tonguing articulation to mute the note. This type of ghosted note will have an audible tone since when half tonguing, the reed does not stop vibrating. This manner of ghosting notes works well at a variety of tempi, especially at very fast speeds when coordination and timing are critical. Since there are a variety of methods used to ghost notes, it is suggested that saxophonists practice each of these approaches to determine which ones work best for them in different performance situations.

SECRET 50: GROWLING

Growling is a technique primarily used by saxophonists when performing commercial and jazz music. This technique changes the timbre of a note, giving it a raspy, growling quality and adding much intensity and expression.

There are two methods of producing a growl on the saxophone. The first method requires the saxophonist to hum while playing a note. It does not matter what pitch is hummed, but it is not usually the same pitch as the note being played and most of the time, the hummed pitch is in the middle to lower range of the voice. The hummed note should be thought of as a drone note that is in a comfortable range for the saxophonist to hum since the pitch of the note is not a factor in producing the growl.

When first attempting to produce a growl, the saxophonist should play a note in the middle register of the instrument. After beginning the note, the saxophonist should then try to hum while not allowing the note to stop. When initially attempting to growl, the saxophonist should increase the pressure and amount of airflow coming from the lungs since the extra pressure and volume will assist in pushing the air past the humming vocal chords. It is also very helpful to hum loudly, as this will make growling easier.

When humming to play a growling note, the saxophonist will be able to hear both the note being played and the note being hummed, which may cause some concern. However, the hummed note will not be audible to the audience members since they will be some distance away from the performer and also the growling note will cover the humming sound created by the voice.

A second method to create a growl, which is not as common as the first, is to allow a small stream of air to escape out of one corner of the mouth while playing. As the air escapes, the saxophonist buzzes the lips at the corner spot where the air is escaping, which will produce a growling sound. Growled notes produced by this method have a slightly different timbre than notes produced by humming and may be preferred by some saxophonists.

Growling is a technique that may be difficult to do at first, but with some practice, most performers are successful at producing a growl either by humming or by buzzing the lips. Some saxophonists use both methods of growling, selecting a particular technique based on the notes being played, the style of music, and the specific performance situation.

SECRET 51: SPLIT TONES

The technique of splitting tones is an advanced technique commonly used by saxophonists in commercial and jazz music. This technique, usually applied to notes in the upper and altissimo register, alters a note's timbre, giving it a raspy, growling quality. This technique is somewhat similar to the growling effect discussed in Secret 50 but is produced without humming or buzzing the lips. There is also a noticeable difference in the timbre of a split tone note that, when compared to other approaches, makes it the preferred technique for many saxophonists. The tone of split tone note is somewhat similar to the tone produced when playing a multiphonic note since a split tone is actually a combination of the same note being sounded in two octaves at once.

Before attempting to produce a split tone in the upper or altissimo register, the saxophonist should first practice playing notes in these registers and producing a pure, clean tone that is in tune. After this is accomplished the process of learning to split tones can be undertaken. To begin, the saxophonist should play the note of choice in a long, sustained manner. To change this note into a split tone note, saxophonists should push the lower jaw forward, taking more reed into the mouth while simultaneously applying more lip pressure into the center or heart of the reed. To assist in producing the split tone, the saxophonist should also increase the air pressure by blowing a narrow, focused, forceful stream of air into the instrument.

It may take some experimentation to determine the correct balance of air pressure, lip pressure, and jaw placement needed to produce a split tone note. It may also be helpful not to use the octave key when initially playing a split tone note especially if the note sounding is clean and pure. Playing upper register and altissimo notes with the octave key not depressed will increase the chances of the note splitting. Some saxophonists find that angling the mouthpiece slightly downward as it enters the mouth also assists in producing a split tone. By doing this the airstream is directed more across the tip of the mouthpiece rather than directly into it.

Other factors that affect the production of split tones are reed strength, mouthpiece design, instrument brand, and the specific fingerings used for upper register notes. Altissimo notes have several fingering options, some of which may be more conducive to producing split tones. Saxophonists should experiment with these fingerings to see if certain ones have a tendency to produce clean tones while others produce split tones.

The split tone technique is a favorite device used by many saxophonists, especially those who perform smooth jazz, rhythm and blues, funk, fusion, and rock. By developing the ability to split tones, saxophonists will be much more adept in playing a wide range of musical styles.

SECRET 52: THE TEXAS WOBBLE

The Texas Wobble is a technique used by many saxophonists especially when performing the blues. This effect is actually a shake starting on the note B♭ that quickly leaps down to the note G a minor third below and then back to B♭ in a tremolo effect. The factor that sets this shake apart from other shakes is the fingerings used. Instead of playing these notes with their normal fingerings, alternate fingerings are used to change their timbres, creating interest, expression, and character.

To produce the Texas Wobble, the saxophonist should first play a B♭ with the octave key depressed, and then the note G located a minor third below, using regular fingerings to get these two pitches into the ear. Next the note B♭ should be played but with an alternate fingering, the fingering for E♭ located a perfect fifth below, but with the left-hand ring finger not depressed. This fingering will produce the B♭ but with a different timbre.

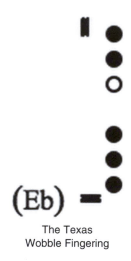

The Texas
Wobble Fingering

To produce the Texas Wobble between B♭ and G, the saxophonist will need to blow a forceful stream of air into the instrument while using an extremely wide and quick jaw vibrato. This vibrato will cause the B♭ note to quickly leap down to a pitch very close to G and then back to B♭. No change in fingering is needed. This technique is definitely enjoyable to play and will produce an interesting and entertaining effect in the music.

SECRET 53: THE CANNONBALL TRILL

The Cannonball Trill is actually a tremolo effect made popular by the great jazz saxophonist Cannonball Adderley. Cannonball, as well as other prominent saxophonists, used this tremolo in many of his solos, especially when improvising on blues tunes. This effect consists of a series of five notes played consecutively with tremolos applied to notes two, three, and four. This technique is note specific and can only be performed using the notes G, B, C, C♮, and D since the tremolos for each note are played with the right-hand index finger using only one alternate fingering, the high E top side key. However, the Cannonball Trill can be performed in the lower and upper register.

To perform the Cannonball Trill, the saxophonist first plays the note G as a pickup note to begin the effect. There is no tremolo applied to this note. The next three notes to be played are B, C, and C♮. When playing these notes, the saxophonist should scoop into each note by slightly dropping the lower jaw and then quickly returning it to its original position while simultaneously depressing and releasing the high E top side key in a trilling fashion. The last note to be played is D, which ends the effect. The saxophonist should also scoop into this note, but tremolo is not applied.

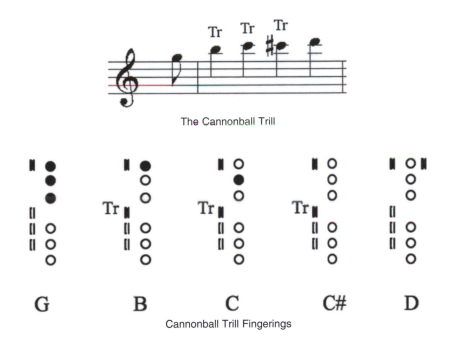

The Cannonball Trill

Cannonball Trill Fingerings

As with any technique, it is highly suggested that saxophonists listen to recordings of performers using this effect and imitate the sound they hear. By listening and using the information presented, the saxophonist should be successful in producing the Cannonball Trill.

SECRET 54: JAZZ VIBRATO

Vibrato is a technique used by most advanced saxophonists to add expression to the music, improve intonation, and allow notes to have a singing quality. Although there are several techniques for producing vibrato, the preferred method for saxophonists is jaw vibrato, which is fully discussed in Secret 27. When examining the use of vibrato in both classical and jazz styles, saxophonists will discover that there are major differences in the way vibrato is played between the two. In order to properly perform vibrato in each of these styles, it is important for saxophonists to know these differences and adjust the style of vibrato accordingly.

Classical Vibrato

When performing classical music, vibrato is usually played on all notes of longer durations unless the performer is instructed otherwise. Classical vibrato is started immediately after the note is begun and has a relatively quick speed. Vibrato in this style has steady, even pulses and a consistent vibrato width. However, vibrato speed and width may vary from one piece to the next or within the same piece, depending upon the style, tempo, and intensity desired. Classical vibrato is considered an essential part of the overall tone and is somewhat standardized in the sense that performers do not use it as a way of individualizing their playing style. Saxophonists who desire to play in the classical style should listen to and imitate the vibrato styles of prominent classical artists performing on a variety instruments, not just the saxophone. By doing this, the saxophonist will soon develop the ability to perform music in this style with the appropriate vibrato.

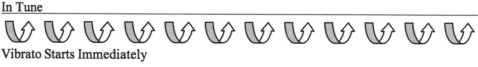

In Tune

Vibrato Starts Immediately

Classical Vibrato

Jazz Vibrato

When playing traditional jazz music, vibrato is used sparingly on medium and fast tempo tunes since performers in this style usually play a straight tone. However, vibrato is frequently used on tunes performed at slower tempi, especially ballads. When playing a ballad, vibrato is usually applied to all notes of longer duration, but unlike classical vibrato, jazz vibrato does not start immediately after the note is begun. Jazz performers prefer to start a note without vibrato, which builds tension in the musical phrase. After the note has sounded for a while, vibrato is applied toward the middle or end of the note, releasing the tension and allowing the note to sing. Also unlike classical vibrato, the speed and width of vibrato may change constantly depending upon the performer's expressive desires. Jazz vibrato is not considered a part of the overall tone and is used to create intensity, expression, and, for some saxophonists, a distinctive performance style.

Jazz Vibrato

Smooth Jazz Vibrato

Smooth jazz is a style of music that has recently gained popularity with a wide range of listeners as well as performers. When performing this style of music, saxophonists use a combination of vibrato techniques from both classical and traditional jazz music. Like classical vibrato, smooth jazz vibrato is usually played on all notes of longer duration and begins immediately after the note is sounded. However, vibrato speed and width may vary greatly between pieces and also between performers as seen in the traditional jazz style. Smooth jazz vibrato is considered a part of the overall tone as in classical music, but many smooth jazz performers also use it as a way to establish their own distinctive sound.

Playing Vibrato in a Variety of Styles

Perhaps the most important factors in learning to play vibrato in a variety of musical styles are listening and imitation. Saxophonists must develop in their minds a concept of how appropriate vibrato sounds in each musical style. This is done by repeatedly listening to recordings of outstanding performers in each musical style, noting differences in vibrato speed, width, and consistency. Then through imitation, the saxophonist can begin to apply the knowledge he or she has learned into performance situations. Through listening and imitation, saxophonists will develop the ability to correctly perform vibrato in many different musical styles.

SECRET 55: OVERTONE FINGERINGS FOR TIMBRE CHANGES

Overtones are often practiced by saxophonists in order to improve tone and throat flexibility and to develop the ability to play in the altissimo register. However, overtones can also be used to provide interesting timbre changes for repeated notes or to add a unique tone quality to specific notes in a musical phrase. Before attempting this technique, the saxophonist should first be proficient at playing the overtone series using low B♭, low B, and low C as fundamental notes as discussed in Secret 37.

To implement this technique, the saxophonist plays the selected note of choice, but instead of using its normal fingering, an overtone fingering is substituted in its place. However, for this to be successful, the saxophonist must be able to hear the desired pitch before it is played and adjust the airstream in such a way that the correct tone is produced with the overtone fingering. This technique is especially effective when playing repeated notes in which normal fingerings and overtone fingerings are alternated between consecutive notes, maximizing their tonal differences as seen below.

Overtone Fingerings for Timbre Changes 1
*Play these notes as overtones using the Low C fingering.
Play all other notes using their regular fingerings.

Overtone Fingerings for Timbre Changes 2
*1 Play this note as an overtone using the Low B♭ fingering.
*2 Play this note as an overtone using the Low C fingering.
Play all other notes using their regular fingerings.

This technique is used by many commercial and jazz performers as a way of adding expression and interest to their solos. It is suggested that saxophonists experiment with this technique, finding interesting and distinctive ways of incorporating it into their playing style.

SECRET 56: USING THE METRONOME IN A JAZZ SWING STYLE

The metronome is an essential tool for improving musicianship. All musicians should practice with a metronome to develop the ability to perform with a steady rhythm and play notes evenly. When using the metronome in classical music, the saxophonist usually places the metronome click on each beat of the measure or sometimes, when playing at slower tempo, on each beat and the upbeat. When performing music in a jazz style, many saxophonists use the metronome in the same manner as when practicing classical literature. However, since performing swing eighth note rhythms in a jazz style is very different than performing even eighth notes in a classical style, it may be helpful for saxophonists to use the metronome in a manner that simulates the jazz rhythm section, allowing them to practice playing swing eighth notes correctly.

When performing with a jazz rhythm section, it is important for saxophonists to listen carefully to the bass line, ride cymbal, and high hat in order to place notes in their correct positions rhythmically and to establish a good swing feel. When practicing alone, saxophonists would greatly benefit if the metronome could be used to simulate these instruments, allowing practice to occur in the most realistic environment possible. Although the metronome cannot reproduce bass line or ride cymbal notes, it can be used to reproduce the high hat, which plays on beats two and four in traditional swing music.

Jazz Metronome Technique

To use this technique, the saxophonist should first practice slowly with the metronome clicking on each beat of the measure. This will ensure the music is being counted correctly and performed accurately. Next the metronome should be set at one-half the speed it was clicking when used on each beat of the measure. For example, if the saxophonist is practicing a piece at a metronome marking of 160 with the metronome clicking on each beat of the measure, the metronome should now be set at 80 to simulate the high hat. With this setting, the metronome is now clicking two times a measure, on beats two and four, in a 4/4 time signature.

Jazz Metronome Technique
Metronome Clicking on Each Beat
Metronome Clicking on Beats 2 and 4

When first attempting this technique, the performer may hear the two metronome clicks as beats one and three, which is exactly opposite of what the high hat plays in a swing style. To correct this, the saxophonist should audibly count along with the metronome to mentally switch the clicks to beats two and four. For example, at the moment the metronome clicks, the saxophonist should repeatedly begin counting to four, starting on the number two. The number two will be with a metronome click, number three will be between metronome clicks, number four will be on a metronome click, and number one will be between metronome clicks. By doing this the metronome will now be clicking on counts two and four of the measure. This process should be used until the performer can naturally hear the metronome on beats two and four.

In addition to using the metronome for practicing scales, chord progressions, patterns, and jazz ensemble music, this method is also very beneficial when practicing an improvised solo. When saxophonists use a metronome clicking on beats two and four, they will begin to develop a stronger swing feel and also perform better with the rhythm section since the drummer's high hat is being simulated in individual practices. It is highly recommended that all jazz saxophonists practice with the metronome in this manner.

CHAPTER 10

Traveling Strategies

SECRET 57: SAXOPHONE GIG BAGS AND CASES

When traveling with a saxophone, it is very important to keep the instrument protected. There are many saxophone gig bags and cases currently being manufactured, all designed to offer protection, convenience, and style to some degree. When performing locally, the method of transporting a saxophone is not nearly as important as when traveling longer distances since the performer has more control over how the instrument is handled and the time traveled is usually short. However, when traveling longer distances, there is a greater chance of instrument damage due to increased travel time and less control over the instrument especially when using public transportation.

Saxophone Gig Bags

When selecting a method to store and transport a saxophone, the first decision to be made is whether to purchase a gig bag or a hard shell case. Gig bags are soft-sided, thickly padded bags designed primarily for convenience and style. These bags are lightweight and have a soft, durable outer shell constructed of nylon, Cordura, or leather. They are held closed with dual zippers and designed with shoulder or backpack straps in addition to handles, making them easy to carry. Gig bags are contoured to fit the form of the saxophone, which makes them small, but they also have built-in pockets to store accessories. Prices for gig bags range from those made of inexpensive nylon to more expensive ones made of leather.

Perhaps the biggest advantages to using a gig bag are its weight and the way it is carried. Anyone who frequently travels will appreciate a bag that is lightweight and also equipped with a shoulder or backpack strap, putting the weight on the back and shoulders while freeing the hands to carry other items. The biggest disadvantage to using a gig bag is protection. Since the bag has a soft outer shell, the only thing protecting the instrument is the thick foam padding sewn in the lining. While this foam may protect against minor bumps, the chance of the instrument being damaged by a major bump, by being dropped, or by something falling on it is greatly increased. Therefore, when using a gig bag, the saxophonist must be very diligent in overseeing the handling of the instrument.

Saxophone Cases

Saxophone hard shell cases are designed primarily for instrument protection but also include other features such as pockets for storage and various approaches for carrying. Hard shell cases are constructed with a variety of rigid exteriors, one of which is wood covered either with vinyl, nylon, or Cordura. Other exteriors are made from polyethylene, or ABS, which is a strong, temperature-resistant plastic that is colorfast and easy to mold. Hard shell cases can be contoured with shoulder or backpack straps or rectangular in shape with briefcase-style handles. If a hard shell case is contoured, storage room may be limited. However, a cover can be purchased for many of these cases that will allow the performer additional storage pockets for accessories. Other options include cases that are closed with dual zippers or latches, and some are even designed with wheels and a telescoping handle.

Like gig bags, hard shell cases range in price from inexpensive wood-and-vinyl construction to more expensive ABS exteriors. The biggest advantage of hard shell cases is the protection they provide. With their rigid exteriors, hard shell cases provide much more protection and peace of mind than gig bags. The biggest disadvantage is the issue of weight. Even when carrying these cases with a shoulder or backpack strap, there is a noticeable difference in weight from that of a gig bag.

Before selecting either a gig bag or a saxophone case, performers should carefully consider their performance needs. If traveling only limited distances to performance venues where saxophonists can monitor their instrument at all times, using a gig bag should be fine. However, when traveling longer distances or in situations where the instrument cannot be personally monitored, a contoured hard shell case is highly recommended. Even though this may be less convenient due to the additional weight, it is well worth the extra effort to arrive at the performance with an instrument that is not damaged.

Protec Contoured Sax Case. *Courtesy of Protecmusic.com*

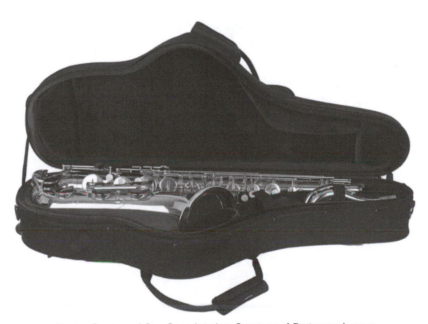

Protec Contoured Sax Case Interior. *Courtesy of Protecmusic.com*

SECRET 58: ITEMS TO KEEP IN THE SAXOPHONE CASE

When traveling, saxophonists must be prepared for unexpected events that could have a negative impact on a performance. Just before going onstage and even while onstage, equipment failure could happen and unless the saxophonist is prepared, the performance may have to be delayed or halted altogether. Although some emergencies cannot be solved no matter how prepared a performer is, by carrying certain items in their case, saxophonists may be able to overcome an unforeseen predicament without any negative consequences occurring.

Items that should be carried pertaining to reeds and reed adjustment are a reed clipper to adjust reeds that are too soft, reed rush, fine-grain sandpaper and a reed knife to adjust reeds that are too hard, a small plastic film canister for soaking reeds, at least eight reeds that are ready to play stored in a reed guard, and a box of reeds.

Other items that are extremely important are two completely assembled mouthpieces with ligatures and reeds, two neck straps, cork grease, a pencil, a set of ear plugs, and a small screwdriver for instrument adjustment. By carrying these items, saxophonists can know they are doing everything possible to avoid performance problems, allowing them to think about more important issues such as making music.

SECRET 59: BOARDING FLIGHTS WITH A SAXOPHONE

On occasion, saxophonists may need to fly to a performance venue when it is not practical or convenient to drive. With increased airport security and new airline baggage policies, boarding an aircraft with a saxophone can cause problems for the performer. However, through careful research and planning, most issues can be avoided.

Types of Larger Aircraft

When planning a flight, it is very important for saxophonists to know the type and size of aircraft they will be traveling on during each leg of their journey since carry-on baggage policies vary from one aircraft to another. This information is posted as part of the flight itinerary and can be easily viewed when browsing for possible flights on an airline's website. Larger aircraft usually pose no problems for saxophonists choosing to carry on an instrument, unless it is a baritone saxophone, and should be used whenever possible. These aircraft are the Airbus A319, A320, and A330; the Boeing 737, 747, 757, 767, and 777; and the McDonnell Douglas MD 88 and MD 90.

Carry-On Baggage

Before booking a flight, saxophonists should review the carry-on baggage restrictions for the airline planning to be used. Most airlines have information on their website devoted to this topic with special information regarding musical instruments. Passengers are allowed one carry-on bag and one personal item such as a briefcase or laptop computer. Carry-on baggage cannot exceed 22" × 14" × 9" on larger aircraft, which allows guitars and smaller musical instruments to be brought into the cabin. Soprano and alto saxophones are allowed as carry-on baggage due to their small case size, and tenor saxophones are allowed as long as they are transported in a contoured saxophone case.

Types of Smaller Aircraft

When flying to or from cities where passenger numbers are fewer, airlines use smaller aircraft for some flights depending upon the flight schedule. Smaller planes are most often used for very early or late flights while larger aircraft are flown at more popular flight times. This information is important because smaller planes have more restrictive carry-on baggage policies, which could present a problem to a saxophonist traveling with an instrument. Since these aircraft are smaller, only items such as small backpacks, briefcases, and laptop computers are allowed in the cabin. Bags that are normally allowed as carry-on items on larger aircraft, including saxophones, are not allowed in the cabin and are required to be gate checked. These smaller planes, which should be avoided if possible when booking a flight, are the Canadair Regional Jet 200 (CRJ), 700 (CR7), and 900 (CR9) and the Embraer 145 (ERJ), 170 (E70), and 175 (E75). When flying to cities where smaller aircraft are used, the saxophonist should carefully examine the flight schedule and try to avoid booking flights that use smaller planes. Sometimes by arriving or departing at a slightly different time, the performer can travel on larger aircraft and avoid carry-on baggage problems.

Gate-Checked Bags

Gate checking a bag refers to taking a carry-on item, labeling it with a special tag, and checking it in at the gate just before boarding the aircraft. Gate-checked bags are placed underneath the plane by airline personnel and do not travel on a conveyor belt like other large bags checked at the airline ticket counter. When arriving at the final destination or when connecting to another flight, the passenger picks up a gate-checked bag at the gate immediately after exiting the aircraft.

Even though gate-checked bags are not treated as roughly as large bags checked at the airline ticket counter, there is still a risk of the instrument being damaged. Once the instrument is turned over to a baggage handler at the gate, the saxophonist has no way to monitor the way it is handled. Saxophonists traveling with an instrument in a hard shell case might be able to sustain no instrument damage, but if a soft shell gig bag is used, major instrument damage is likely. Saxophonists should avoid having their instrument gate checked if possible by booking flights that use large aircraft.

Selecting Seats and Packing for Travel

When selecting a seat for the upcoming flight, the performer should choose a seat close to the rear of the aircraft since in many instances the plane is boarded from the rear first. By doing this, the saxophonist will be one of the first on board, with the exception of business class, and have plenty of overhead compartment to stow his or her instrument.

When packing for the trip, the saxophone should be placed in a hard shell contoured case equipped with either shoulder or backpack straps. Key clamps should be used to restrict key movement, and the instrument should be wrapped in a soft cloth to limit its movement inside the case. Never use a gig bag with a soft outer shell to transport a saxophone when flying. If saxophonists wish to check their instrument as baggage, a heavy-duty Anvil case is highly recommended.

Passing through Security

When preparing to pass through airport security with a saxophone, the performer can expect to receive extra scrutiny. Many times an explosive residue test is performed on the saxophone case, especially if flying internationally. This test consists of swabbing the inside of the saxophone case and performing an analysis of the results to see if any explosive material has been in contact with the case. Saxophonists should also remove any reed knives from their saxophone case before leaving for the airport, packing them in their checked baggage. If this is not done, there will be a problem with security since reed knives are not allowed in the cabin. Screwdrivers for adjusting the instrument are allowed as long as they are not longer than seven inches.

Boarding an Aircraft with a Saxophone

When approaching the gate to board the aircraft, remember that gate agents and flight attendants are the ones in charge of carry-on items and determine what is allowed in the cabin and what is not. Some agents are very strict while others are not. A carry-on item may be allowed on one flight and the same item on the same type of aircraft may not be allowed on another, depending upon the gate agent and flight crew.

When boarding a flight, saxophonists should not draw attention to their instrument. The instrument should always be carried over the shoulder with a shoulder strap or on the back using backpack straps, hiding as much of the case as possible. Performers should never carry it by the handles at their side as this is easily seen. If a saxophonist is told the instrument will need to be gate checked, permission to carry the instrument on board may be granted by nicely speaking with the gate agent, flight attendant, or both before boarding the flight. Explaining to the agent that the passenger is on the way to a performance and the instrument, which is worth several thousand dollars, will be damaged if gate checked will greatly improve the chances of getting permission to carry the instrument on board.

When entering the aircraft, saxophonists should keep the instrument behind them until passing by the flight attendants at the front of the plane. Once this is done, the instrument should be carried in front of the body to further hide it while finding the assigned seat. When reaching the seat, the instrument should be stowed in the overhead compartment and boarding a flight with a saxophone has been accomplished. It is hoped that these suggestions will assist saxophonists in flying with the least amount of problems while keeping their instrument safe.

SECRET 60: PRACTICE AND PERFORMANCE TIPS

Before traveling to a concert venue, there are steps saxophonists can take to adequately prepare them for the performance. These steps include correct practice procedures used to prepare the music before a concert and also performance routines to be followed at the time of the concert. Being properly prepared will increase the quality of a performance and also allow saxophonists to thoroughly enjoy their time onstage.

Practice Strategies

The first step is to know how to practice. Often saxophonists practice lengthy sections of music, playing them too quickly and making many mistakes. After continually practicing the music incorrectly, the performer may actually play the piece with no mistakes and decide to move on to another piece. However, this method of practicing could lead to a disastrous performance since the music was played incorrectly many more times than correctly. To correctly practice, saxophonists should divide a musical piece into small, manageable sections, which are played slowly and perfectly every time with a metronome. As the performer masters the material, the tempo is slowly increased over a period of time until performance tempo is reached. After the saxophonist can correctly play each section of the piece separately, these sections can be linked together, allowing the entire piece to be performed with no mistakes. Perfect practice makes a perfect performance.

After each musical piece can be correctly performed using the above method, it is time to practice the entire program as it would be played on the concert date. Many saxophonists skip this step, only performing the entire program at the actual concert. However, by skipping this step, saxophonists may experience problems during the performance since factors such as endurance and mental concentration are not tested until the concert date. To correctly practice, the saxophonist should play the entire concert in order, simulating the performance as closely as possible. After playing the program, the performer can then practice sections of each piece that need more work. This procedure should be completed once each day for at least a week prior to the performance. By doing this, the saxophonist should feel very comfortable onstage during the performance. Amateur performers practice a piece of music until they can play it right; professional performers practice a piece of music until they cannot play it wrong.

Performance Routines

There are other routines that saxophonists can employ immediately prior to the performance to make sure things go smoothly. The first is to arrive early at the venue to inspect the stage and room conditions. Warm up while testing to see which reed works best in the room and to make sure the instrument is working properly. The saxophonist should have at least eight reeds that are broken in and numbered showing their ranking from best to worst. Sometimes when warming up, the saxophonist will discover that the number one reed does not play as well as other lower-ranked reeds due to room conditions. Next, tune the saxophone using a tuner and perform a brief section of the program to become familiar with the acoustics of the room. It is now time to take a break and get dressed for the performance. It is suggested that the saxophonist not eat a large meal before a performance because this may affect breathing and other performance abilities. However, if nervousness or performance anxiety is a problem, eating a banana 30 minutes prior to performing may help calm the performer down since bananas are natural beta blockers that reduce the amount of adrenaline absorbed by certain parts of the body. When it is time to perform, tune backstage and then walk confidently onstage ready to make music.

shake, 114
shell, 11
Sigurd Rascher mouthpiece, 7
slap tonguing, 97
smooth jazz, 117
sore lip, 51; braces, 53; causes, 51; inside, 52; outside, 51
split tone, 113
spoiler, 10
sub-toning, 103
swing eighth notes, 104
swinging, 104–105

teeth marks, 52–53
Texas Wobble, 114
throat, 66–67

tone, 4–6, 9–10, 61, 68; classical, 5–6, 28; jazz, 9–10; overtone exercise for improving, 68; tongue position, 65
tonguing patterns, 73–74
traveling, 125
triple tonguing, 75–77
tremolo, 115

vacuum, 36
Vandoren, 6, 14, 17, 27, 37
vibrato, 70–71; classical, 70, 116; developing, 70; jazz, 116–118; speed, 70–71; width, 70–71
voicing, 11

Yamaha, 1–2, 14

About the Author

Tracy Lee Heavner is an internationally known music educator and distinguished performance artist for Cannonball, Yamaha, and Beechler music corporations. He currently serves on the faculty at the University of South Alabama as a professor of music education and saxophone and as director of jazz studies. Dr. Heavner completed degrees in music education from the University of Northern Colorado (D.M.E.) and Appalachian State University (M.M.E., B.M.E.). He is a recording artist for LiveHorns and has performed throughout the United States and abroad, including Carnegie Hall, the World Saxophone Congress, and the Montreux Jazz Festival. His professional endeavors in music research have produced publications in numerous juried music journals, and he has presented research at conferences across the United States and at international conferences around the world.